RAF Benson

RAF Benson
A diary of wartime losses

Reginald H. Ottaway

SPEEDMAN PRESS LIMITED

First published in Great Britain in 2010 by
Speedman Press Ltd

Copyright © R.H. Ottaway, 2010
ISBN 978-0-9562176-1-5

The right of R.H. Ottaway to be identified as author of this work has been asserted by him in accordance with the Copyright, Designs and Patents Act 1988.

A CIP catalogue record for this book is available from the British Library

All rights reserved. No part of this book may be reproduced or transmitted in any form or by any means, electronic or mechanical including photocopying, recording or by any information storage and retrieval system, without permission from the publisher in writing.

Typeset in Palatino Linotype and Gill Sans by
Lamorna Publishing Services

Printed in Great Britain by the MPG Books Group,
Bodmin and King's Lynn

Speedman Press Ltd
Speedman House
Andover
Hampshire
SP10 4LW
England
E-mail: enquiries@speedmanpress.co.uk
Website: www.speedmanpress.co.uk

Contents

Introduction .... *vii*
Preface .... *viii*
Acknowledgements .... *ix*
Illustrations .... *x*
Units .... *xiv*
Abbreviations .... *xv*

1939 1
1940 5
1941 10
1942 35
1943 63
1944 96
1945 128

Appendices

I   Summary of Aircraft Losses 136
II   No. 8 (Coastal) Operational Training Unit 138
III   RAF Station Benson Commanders 1939 – 1945 145
IV   List of Honours and Awards 146
V   Brief History of PR since 1939 151
VI   Notes on the Work of PR Squadrons 159
VII   RAF Station Benson personnel and others buried in St Helen's Churchyard Extension, Benson 164
VIII RAF Station Benson personnel commemorated on the Runnymede Memorial 166
IX   RAF Station Benson Gate Guardian 173

Sources 182
Index 183

Introduction

RAF Benson: A diary of wartime losses was both a labour of love and an ongoing project for my late father, Reg Ottaway.

In 1981 he presented the first, typewritten edition of the book to Group Captain A. Mumford, the station commander, for the library at RAF Benson. His research did not stop there and he updated the volume several times.

Sometime after his death we found other information amongst his papers which suggested he was planning another update. I decided to edit the book for publication and have included the extra facts that he did not have the chance to add to his original work. Since I was not sure how he intended all of them to be shown, many of them now appear as appendices.

In the years since Dad's death it has become more straightforward to access information than it was when he did his research and certain facts that would have been very difficult for him to collect are now much easier to find. Had he lived longer I believe he would have wanted to include the details, where known, of the fate of those airmen who failed to return from their sorties and so, as far as possible, I have added them to the book. I hope he would have approved.

Susan Ottaway

Preface

Royal Air Force Station Benson lies nestled within the rolling hills of Oxfordshire, situated approximately 15 miles from the city of Oxford and two miles from Wallingford, surrounded by small picturesque villages in peaceful countryside.

Although the same villages were to be found there during the period 1939 – 1945 the peace and tranquillity was replaced by the urgency of wartime when RAF Station Benson became a hive of aviation activity.

This diary is not intended to be a day by day record of these activities, but a diary of events and losses recorded as they occurred in and around RAF Station Benson and its satellite stations.

Some items prefixed RAF Station Benson do not necessarily refer to any station incident, but the information recorded has been extracted from RAF Station Benson's Operations Record Book for that period.

Ranks and decorations do not always include any posthumous promotions or awards.

Whilst every endeavour has been made to include all units, their losses and events, any omissions are purely accidental, for which I apologise.

Acknowledgements

My appreciation to all staff of the Public Records Office (now the National Archives) at Kew, Surrey, as without their cooperation this work would not have been possible. Transcripts of Crown copyright records in the National Archives appear by permission of the controller of HM Stationery Office.

To Mr Jack Radford at the Runnymede Air Forces Memorial.

To my family for their encouragement and assistance.

To Royal Air Force Station Benson for the happy memories I have as a FMA at this station during the period 1939-1945.

R.H. Ottaway

Illustrations

1. Building work at Benson *(via Robin Brooks)* xviii
2. RAF construction workers *(via Robin Brooks)* xviii
3. 'C' type hangars *(via Robin Brooks)* xix
4. Benson aerodrome in 1940 *(via Robin Brooks)* xx
5. The KCB filling station *(via Robin Brooks)* xx
6. Fairey Battles *(via RAF Benson History Room)* 4
7. Vickers Wellington *(via RAF Benson History Room)* 9
8. Flying Officer Dowse *(via RAF Benson History Room)* 16
9. HRH the Duke of Kent and F/O W. Panton *(G.W. Puttick via RAF Benson History Room)* 16
10. Camouflaged Spitfire *(via RAF Benson History Room)* 18
11. German heavy cruiser *Prinz Eugen* *(via Martin Bowman)* . .18
12. The chapel at RAF Benson *(via RAF Benson History Room)* .21
13. F/O M. Suckling *(via RAF Benson History Room)* 21
14. F/O Greenhill *(via RAF Benson History Room)* 24
15. F/O Blair *(via RAF Benson History Room)* 24
16. F/O Harding and friends *(via RAF Benson History Room)* . .24
17. Sir Archibald Sinclair *(via RAF Benson History Room)* 28
18. 1 PRU 'B' Flight ground crew *(G.W. Puttick via RAF Benson History Room)* 28
19. Wg Cdr G.W. Tuttle *(via RAF Benson History Room)* 31
20. Sqn Ldr A.L. Taylor *(via Martin Bowman)* 31
21. Long-range fuel tanks *(via Martin Bowman)* 36
22. P/O Gunn *(via RAF Benson History Room)* 36
23. F/O A. Densham *(via RAF Benson History Room)* 40
24. P/O F.J. Blackwood *(via RAF Benson History Room)* 40
25. P/O C.D. Harris St John *(via RAF Benson History Room)* . . .47

26. General Sir Bernard C.T. Paget
    (via RAF Benson History Room) 47
27. P/O E.F. Lucarotti *(via RAF Benson History Room)* 52
28. Visiting American B-17 *(via RAF Benson History Room)* 52
29. F/L M.D. Hood *(via RAF Benson History Room)* 57
30. Sqn Ldr A.E. Hill *(via RAF Benson History Room)* 57
31. PR Mosquito camera installation
    (via RAF Benson History Room) 59
32. Film cassette *(via RAF Benson History Room)* 59
33. Toulon PR picture *(via Martin Bowman)* 61
34. Pilots of 'A' Flight 541 Squadron
    (via RAF Benson History Room) 61
35. Crashed Spitfire *(Hugh Rigby via Robin Rigby)* 66
36. F/O D. Croy and friends *(Hugh Rigby via Robin Rigby)* 66
37. Mosquito I W4060 *(via Martin Bowman)* 67
38. Sqn Ldr van der Heijden *(via RAF Benson History Room)* ...67
39. Sgt J. Lavender
    (G.W. Puttick via RAF Benson History Room) 67
40. 542 Squadron circa 1943 *(Mrs J. Fray via Andrew Jenkins)* ..70
41. Sgt R.M. Lawrence
    (G.W. Puttick via RAF Benson History Room) 70
42. Six members of 542 Squadron
    (via RAF Benson History Room) 73
43. RAF Benson Dramatic Society
    (Squadron Leader F.G. Fray) 79
44. Sqn Ldr D. Salwey *(via RAF Benson History Room)* 79
45. Sgt V.I. Gorrill
    (G.W. Puttick via RAF Benson History Room) 82
46. F/O W.R. Acott *(via RAF Benson History Room)* 82
47. The Old Mansion, Ewelme
    (via RAF Benson History Room) 91
48. Photographic Intelligence buildings
    (via RAF Benson History Room) 91
49. Photographic Intelligence staff
    (via RAF Benson History Room) 92
50. Sqn Ldr Smith Lewis *(via RAF Benson History Room)* 92
51. Photographic Intelligence room
    (via RAF Benson History Room) 93

52. Tea break for ground crews
    (via RAF Benson History Room) 93
53. Spitfire XI EN154 *(via Robin Brooks)* 95
54. 'B' Flight of 541 Squadron
    (G.W. Puttick via RAF Benson History Room) 95
55. Operations room at Benson
    (via RAF Benson History Room) 97
56. The Debriefing room at Benson
    (via RAF Benson History Room) 97
57. Mosquito PR IX *(via Martin Bowman)* 101
58. Graves of German airmen
    (Bernie Barton via Steve Rogers, Project Coordinator, The War Graves
    Photographic Project) 101
59. F/O G.W. Puttick
    (G.W. Puttick via RAF Benson History Room) 106
60. Farm at Preston Crowmarsh
    (Mrs J. Fray via Andrew Jenkins) 106
61. Rubber models of D-Day landing beaches
    (via Robin Brooks) 111
62. Danesfield House, RAF Medmenham
    (via RAF Benson History Room) 111
63. F/L J. Weaver *(via RAF Benson History Room)* 116
64. ASO D. Britain *(via RAF Benson History Room)* 116
65. ASO Weightman *(via RAF Benson History Room)* 117
66. ASOs Thompson and Chalmers
    (via RAF Benson History Room) 117
67. ASO Laws *(via RAF Benson History Room)* 117
68. Processing photographs *(via RAF Benson History Room)* . .119
69. 541 Squadron Dispersal *(via Robin Brooks)* 127
70. 544 Squadron couriers for Operation Haycock
    (G.W. Puttick via RAF Benson History Room) 129
71. F/L J. Robson and F/O F. Adlam *(via Robin Brooks)* 132
72. German battleship *Tirpitz* *(Martin Bowman)* 132
73. F/O N.J. Bonnar *(via RAF Benson History Room)* 150
74. F/O G.E. Hughes *(via RAF Benson History Room)* 150
75. F/L P.H. Watts *(via RAF Benson History Room)* 150
76. St Helen's Churchyard Extension, Benson
    (Nick Randall) 165

77. Real Spitfire EN343 *(author's collection)* 175
78. Replica Spitfire EN343 and commemorative plaque
    (Ian Ottaway) 175
79. G/C P. G. Pinney and S/L F. G. Fray *(Ian Ottaway)* 180
80. Author's wife, author, S/L F. G. Fray and F/L G. W. Puttick
    (Ian Ottaway) 180
81. S/L F.G. Fray and replica Spitfire EN343
    (Ian Ottaway) 181

Cover photos *(author's collection)*
Cover designed by Ian A. Ottaway

Thanks to the following for their help with the illustrations: aviation authors Martin Bowman and Robin Brooks for lending photos from their collections; Mrs Janet Fray for lending photos from her late husband's collection; Andrew Jenkins for scanning some of Mrs Fray's photos; Ian Ottaway for the photos of the unveiling of the replica Spitire gate guardian and for the cover design; Robin Rigby for supplying two photos from the collection of his father, Hugh Rigby, the OC No. 4 Air Liaison Section, attached to 140 Squadron during the Second World War; Steve Rogers, Project Coordinator, The War Graves Photographic Project for supplying the photos of the German airmen's grave; Anne Williams of Ewelme for identifying some of the men in the photos; Bill Williams, former Benson PR Spitfire pilot, for checking the identities of those who could not otherwise be identified.

   Finally, special thanks are due to Mick Prendergast of the RAF Benson History Room for his time and endless patience searching for, and supplying, so many of the photos in this book.

Units Included

RAF Station Benson
No. 12 OTU [Operational Training Unit]
52 Squadron
63 Squadron
140 Squadron
170 Squadron
309 FT and ADU
540 Squadron
541 Squadron
542 Squadron
543 Squadron
544 Squadron
1416 Flight (Later changed to 140 Squadron)
PRU (Later changed to No. 1 PRU)
No. 1 PRU
PRDU Benson

Satellite Stations mentioned include:
RAF Station Gibraltar
RAF Station Leuchars
RAF Station Mount Farm
RAF Station St Eval
RAF Station Wick

Abbreviations used in the text

(*Some ranks have been abbreviated in more than one way. This is how they were shown originally in official documents and these differences have been retained. Each explanation is shown here.*)

AA	ack-ack (anti-aircraft gun, fire etc.)
AASF	Advanced Air Striking Force
A/C	aircraft
AC	Aircraftman
AC1	Aircraftman 1st class
AC2	Aircraftman 2nd class
ACW	Aircraftwoman
Air Cdre	Air Commodore
AOC	Air Officer Commanding
ASO	Assistant Section Officer
ASI	air speed indicator
AUW	all up weight
BEF	British Expeditionary Force
CB	Companion of the Most Honourable Order of the Bath
CBE	Commander of the Most Excellent Order of the British Empire
C.-in-C.	Commander in Chief
C/L	crash landed
CMG	Companion of the Most Distinguished Order of St Michael & St George
CO	Commanding Officer
Cpl	Corporal

CRU	Civilian Repair Unit
D/A	damage assessment
DFC	Distinguished Flying Cross
DFM	Distinguished Flying Medal
DSC	Distinguished Service Cross
DSO	Distinguished Service Order
Fg Off	Flying Officer
Flt Lt	Flight Lieutenant
FMA	Flight Mechanic (Airframe)
FME	Flight Mechanic (Engine)
F/O	Flying Officer
FS	Flight Sergeant
F/Sgt	Flight Sergeant
FT and ADU	Ferry Training and Aircraft Dispatch Unit
FTR	failed to return
HE	high explosive (bomb)
HQ	headquarters
IFF	identification, friend or foe
KCB	Knight Commander of the Order of the Bath
KT	Knight of the Most Ancient & Most Noble Order of the Thistle
MC	Military Cross
MO	Medical Officer
MP	Member of Parliament
MTB	Motor Torpedo Boat
MU	Maintenance Unit
MVO	Member of the Royal Victorian Order
OBE	Officer of the Most Excellent Order of the British Empire
OTU	Operational Training Unit
PAF	Polish Air Force

Plt Off	Pilot Officer
P/O	Pilot Officer
PRU	Photographic Reconnaissance Unit
PRDU	Photographic Reconnaissance Development Unit
PT	physical training
RAAF	Royal Australian Air Force
RAE	Royal Aircraft Establishment
RAFVR	Royal Air Force Volunteer Reserve
RCAAF	Royal Canadian Auxiliary Air Force
recce	reconnaissance
RNorAF	Royal Norwegian Air Force
RNZAF	Royal New Zealand Air Force
R/T	radio telegraphy
SAAF	South African Air Force
Sgt	Sergeant
s/n	service number
S/No.	serial number
SOA	Senior Officer Administration
Sqn Ldr	Squadron Leader
U/S	unserviceable
USAAF	United States Army Air Force
Wg Cdr	Wing Commander
W/O	Warrant Officer
W/T	wireless telegraphy

Building work on the airfield at Benson began in 1937 on land purchased from four farmers – Edwards, Orpwood, Chamberlain and Wilder – for £18 per acre. Here workers from Walter Wilder and Sons' farm are gathering in the final harvest.

RAF construction workers in 1938 taking a short break during the building of the aerodrome.

'C' type hangars being built during 1939.

Benson aerodrome in 1940. The runways were still grass at this time.

The KCB – Keep the Country Beautiful – filling station and restaurant which was run by the Horsfield family from 1934 until 1942 when it was demolished to allow for the building of extended concrete runways.

*DEDICATED TO ALL THOSE
WHO
FAILED TO RETURN*

1939

18 September 1939

Nos. 52 and 63 Squadrons proceeded to RAF Station Benson. As a result of a conference held between the Station Commander, Group Captain C.W. Mackey, and the officers commanding Nos. 52 and 63 Squadrons, it was decided that a station training programme should be introduced; the syllabus divided into elementary and advanced operational training. The scheme provides that No. 63 Squadron should be responsible for elementary training, and No. 52 Squadron should be responsible for the advanced training; about three weeks to be spent by trainees in each squadron. The intention of the scheme is for the training of an intake of pilots, air observers, and air gunners from their appropriate schools, giving them an intensive course of six weeks' training to produce personnel fit for operational squadrons. Aircraft to be used are Fairey Battles and Avro Ansons.

6 October 1939

In order to maintain a high standard of aircraft serviceability, a pool of maintenance personnel of Nos. 52 and 63 Squadrons was formed under the command of Squadron Engineering Officer Flying Officer Robbins to carry out major inspections and repairs.

23 October 1939   52 Squadron 'A' Flight

Pilot Officer J.R. Anderson and Aircraftman 1st Class R.A.W. Keogh were killed in a flying accident, caused by a collision during formation flying. This was the first fatal accident sustained by the squadron since it was reformed after the war of 1914-1918 on 18 January 1937. [The Commonwealth War Graves Commission lists the deaths as being on 18 October 1939.]

John Ross Anderson, s/n 41647; age 26. Died on 23 October 1939 and is buried in Oxford (Botley) Cemetery.

Robert Allan Walker Keogh, s/n 569519; age 20; adopted son of Madge G. Keogh of Holdenhurst, Bournemouth, Hampshire. Died on 23 October 1939 and is buried in Benson (St Helen) Churchyard Extension.

29 October 1939

Fairey Battle of combined training unit K9397 crashed today but the crew escaped uninjured.

3 November 1939   63 Squadron

At 1020 hours a fatal accident occurred at Checkendon, a little village in the Chiltern Hills, to Fairey Battle P2274 belonging to 'B' Flight. Pilot Officer George Francis Barwell, the pilot and sole occupant, was killed instantly when his aircraft struck a clump of trees on emerging from very low cloud. The aircraft did not catch fire. The pilot had previously been engaged in formation flying practice and had lost sight of his leader while descending through cloud. He appears to have gone above the cloud again and then descended through a gap when he thought he was somewhere near the aerodrome. He was actually over the Chilterns where the clouds were practically on the ground. The other pilot in the same formation also lost his leader at the same moment and acted in a similar manner to Pilot Officer Barwell. He was more fortunate, however, and although he crashed in a field about a mile away from where Pilot Officer Barwell was killed, he sustained only minor injuries.

Pilot Officer Barwell was given a Service funeral and was buried in Bournemouth.

George Francis Astley Barwell, s/n 41817, age 19, son of Edwin and Gladys Barwell of Bournemouth. Died on 3 November 1939 and is buried in Bournemouth East Cemetery.

1 December 1939　　　　　63 Squadron

Anson N5073 took-off from RAF Benson at 0930 with the following personnel on board – Pilot Officer C.R. Coventry, pilot and captain: Pilot Officer A. Cameron, pupil pilot: Sergeant A.G. Gibson, pupil observer: Aircraftman Second Class H.O.W. Gormlay, pupil air gunner: Aircraftman Second Class J.C. Buckland, pupil air gunner.

The pilot was detailed to carry out a navigation training flight from Benson to Bude in Cornwall, thence to a point 50 miles out to sea and back to make a landfall at Trevose Head, finally returning to Benson. The weather was expected to be bad at the coast and the pilot was told to turn back if he ran into bad weather. Another pilot in a different Anson but engaged on the same duty, did actually turn back when he reached Bude and reported that the clouds were right down on the sea. It is probable that Pilot Officer Coventry attempted to go out to sea and then lost control and dived into the water. He may have encountered severe icing conditions.

In case the missing Anson may have crashed on a lonely hillside and not at sea, a search of Bodmin Moor, Dartmoor, and Exmoor was carried out. Six Ansons took part in the search but no trace was found of the missing Anson. RAF Station St Eval reported that a rubber dinghy and three small portions of an Anson fuselage have been washed up near to Boscastle but there is no positive identification of the aircraft to which they belong.

James Crompton Buckland, s/n 619734, age 19. Son of James and Alice Buckland of Rochdale Lancashire. Died on 1 December 1939 and is commemorated on the Runnymede memorial.

Angus Cameron, s/n 41900, age 22. Son of Angus and Adelaide Cameron of Weston, Ontario, Canada. Died on 1 December 1939 and is commemorated on the Runnymede memorial.

Charles Robey Coventry, s/n 40606, age 27. Son of Charles and Alice Coventry of Brighton, South Australia. Died on 1 December 1939 and is commemorated on the Runnymede memorial.

Alvin Gordon Gibson, s/n 581212, age 19. Son of Flight Lieutenant Frederick and Edith Gibson of Brentford, Middlesex. Died on 1 December 1939 and is commemorated on the Runnymede memorial.

Hugh Oliver Wilson Gormlay, s/n 543996, age 21. Son of Peter and Jane Gormlay of Ilford, Essex. Died on 1 December 1939 and is commemorated on the Runnymede memorial.

Fairey Battles in formation.

1940

31 January 1940　　　　　　**RAF Station Benson**

The 4th Battalion Northamptonshire Regiment took over vulnerable point guard duties from the 6th Battalion Royal Berkshire Regiment. The 90 Light Anti-Aircraft Brigade now have four double Lewis gun posts established in commanding positions around the aerodrome, to defend the station against low flying enemy aircraft.

1 February 1940　　　　　　**RAF Station Benson**

A new scheme for leave is introduced at the Station. It has been found that the system whereby flights have days off at different times does not work very well in practice. It was found that the three day periods of leave to each flight every six weeks interfered with efficient working. Since one group of personnel had a day off every other day, it was seldom possible to get everyone together for a conference or for the purpose of issuing orders. It has now been decided that the whole station shall work on a six day week basis and, in addition, shall have one weekend leave period a month from after duty on a Friday until midnight on Sunday. This system of closing down by squadrons instead of by flights enables the CO and orderly room staff to have time off without the difficulty of havings parts of the squadron working while the HQ is closed.

12 February 1940　　　　　　**52 Squadron**

The Squadron undertook the training of Fairey Battle pilots for the AASF in France, in the spraying of gas from bottles. 'C' Flight was detailed to supply the aircraft while 'A' and 'B' Flights continued with their normal operational training. Pilots were sent from France in courses of twelve and each course stayed two days.

15 February 1940   52 Squadron
Fairey Battle K9460 crashed.
Fairey Battles K9393 and P2271 force landed; machines intact except for damage to P2271 flaps.

29 February 1940   52 Squadron
Fairey Battle K9406 crashed, crew uninjured.
Fairey Battle K9403 Force landed.

1 March 1940   RAF Station Benson
No. 2 Component Field Force formed at Benson under the command of Air Commodore A.J. Capel DSO, DFC for special duties but was disbanded on 31 March 1940.

4 March 1940   RAF Station Benson
The AOC.-in-C. Bomber Command decided to keep his aircraft at Benson where it has been housed with the King's Flight.

6 April 1940   52 Squadron
No. 52 Squadron was this day reduced to number only (disbanded).

Mid-April 1940
Nos. 52 and 63 Squadrons lost their identity and their personnel merged with HQ to form No. 12 OTU. The OTU consists of three wings – HQ, Training and Maintenance, responsible respectively for administration, flying and servicing. The Officer Commanding is to be Group Captain W.H. Dunn DSC.

29-30 June 1940   RAF Station Benson
Enemy aircraft dropped 18 HE bombs in the vicinity of the aerodrome. The attack was from high level and occurred during night flying while the aerodrome was illuminated by full lighting. No casualties or damage was sustained within the

station boundaries. The attack was a complete surprise and no warning was given.

19 July 1940   12 OTU
At 1605 hours His Majesty the King visited 12 OTU. He inspected many different sections and stayed to tea.

13 August 1940   RAF Station Benson
One Ju 88 dived out of cloud at between 2,500-3,000 feet and dropped four bombs: three HE and one oil incendiary. No casualties were incurred but one wing of an Anson was damaged. The attack was a complete surprise and the aircraft took cover above cloud immediately.

13 August 1940   12 OTU
The first Polish trainees arrived.

14 August 1940   Mount Farm
The satellite aerodrome at Mount Farm, Drayton St Leonards is making good progress with the construction of concrete runways which should be finished by the end of September.

26 August 1940   RAF Station Benson
Marshal of the Royal Air Force the Viscount Trenchard visited the station today.

26 August 1940   12 OTU
Forty Czech pilots arrived for grading as to suitability for fighter pilots.

27 August 1940   RAF Station Benson
Discussions have proceeded during the month as to the function of Benson, on the reorganization of OTU and the provision of perimeter tracks and the taxi tracks for the aerodrome. No final decisions were arrived at.

30 September 1940   12 OTU
Fairey Battle I L5079 lost engine power and hit trees on high ground while trying to make a belly landing near Streatley in Berkshire during a training flight. The aircraft was destroyed by fire. The pilot, Warrant Officer O. Odstrcilek, was killed.

Otakar Odstrcilek, s/n 787369, age 29. Czechoslovak national born on 9 December 1910 in Osvetim, Poland. Died on 30 September 1940 and was buried in Benson (St Helen) Churchyard Extension on 4 October 1940.

1 October 1940   12 OTU

Pilot Officer J.M.R. de Jenko-Sokolowski, on a solo flight in Fairey Battle I K9416, crashed at 2030 hours in woods near Checkendon, Oxfordshire, east of Wallingford. The reason for the crash is not known.

Jerzy Marian Ryszard de Jenko-Sokolowski, PAF, s/n P1360, age 32. Born on 25 November 1907. Died on 1 October 1940 and is buried in Benson (St Helen) Churchyard Extension.

3 October 1940   RAF Station Benson

The Air Officer in Command No. 6 Group visited the station today. [Air Vice-Marshal W.F. MacN. Foster CB, CBE, DSO, DFC]

24 October 1940   RAF Station Benson

One instance of air attack; two HE bombs were dropped but exploded in an adjoining field.

26 November 1940   12 OTU

Fairey Battle L5071 took-off from Mount Farm at 1930 hours but minutes later crashed one mile north-west of the airfield. The aircraft burnt out. The crew, Flying Officer W. Makarewicz, (pilot), Flying Officer A. Ignaszak (observer) and Leading Aircraftman F. Blyskal (air gunner), all Poles, were killed.

Wladyslaw Makarewicz, PAF, s/n P0063, age 25. Born on 25 March 1915. Died on 26 November 1940 and is buried in Benson (St Helen) Churchyard Extension.

Antoni Ignaszak, PAF, s/n P0071, age 27. Born on 24 February 1913. Died on 26 November 1940 and is buried in Benson (St Helen) Churchyard Extension.

Franciszek Blyskal, s/n 793314, age 20. Born on 10 January 1920. Having trained as a gunner, he left Poland and eventually reached France from where he was evacuated to the United Kingdom in 1940 and joined the RAF. He died on 26 November 1940 and is buried in Benson (St Helen) Churchyard Extension.

1 December 1940   **12 OTU**

With effect from 1 December 1940 No. 12 OTU is reduced from medium bomber OTU (Battles) to half heavy bombers OTU (Wellingtons).

27 December 1940   **PRU**

PRU started the move from Heston to Benson; the move was officially timed to take four days with operational flights starting from Benson on 27 December 1940. The aerodrome at Benson was found to be very soft and operations are being carried out from the satellite at Dorchester (Mount Farm).

27 December 1940   **PRU**

Sergeant Mills in Spitfire P9550 force landed near Bexhill owing to bad visibility after returning from an operation. Take-off was at 1315 hours and the aircraft crash landed at 1550 hours.

Vickers Wellington of 12 OTU.

1941

13 January 1941   RAF Station Benson
The Commander in Chief Coastal Command Sir Frederick W. Bowhill KCB CMG DSO, Air Vice Marshal G.R. Bromet DSO OBE, senior Air Staff Officer and Wing Commander Strain DSC OBE visited the station and inspected various branches of PRU. They were taken round by Wing Commander Tuttle DFC OBE, then stayed for lunch.

18 January 1941   PRU
Flight Lieutenant J.S.D. Miles took-off in Spitfire I for an operation over enemy territory and FTR (failed to return). The Operations Book Form 540 gives no other details.

John Stuart Dixon Miles s/n 28002 age 31. son of Stanley and Mabel Miles, husband of Joan Richmond Miles of Endmoor Westmorland. Died on 18 January 1941 and is buried in Marquise Communal Cemetery, France.

26 January 1941   RAF Station Benson
Squadron Leader Beresford DFC and Flight Lieutenant Spender took-off in a Tiger Moth from Chivenor for Benson but owing to bad weather put down in a field. Squadron Leader Beresford then left Flight Lieutenant Spender in the field and took-off for the aerodrome but had to bale out.

30 January 1941   PRU St Eval detachment
A number of enemy aircraft attacked the aerodrome at dusk and dropped HE bombs, one of which hit a shelter causing eight fatal casualties but none to PRU personnel.

30 January 1941   RAF Station Benson

Enemy aircraft dropped 19 HE bombs, 50-150lbs in weight, and three incendiaries along the east side of the aerodrome; no casualties or damage.

12 February 1941   Mount Farm

Aircraftman 2nd Class A.W.R. Mallett was killed by the airscrew of a Wellington.

Albert Walter Richard Mallett, s/n 921945, age 24, son of Albert and Emily Mallett of Littleton. Died on 12 February 1941 and is buried in Littleton (St Catherine) Churchyard Extension.

16 February 1941   PRU

Pilot Officer J.D. Chandler in Spitfire PR III P9561, failed to return from a Spitfire sortie to Ostend. The Operations Book Form 540 gives no other details.

John Derek Chandler RAFVR, s/n 79518, son of Hugh and Ethel Chandler of Witley, Surrey. Died on 16 February 1941 and is commemorated on the Runnymede Memorial.

21 February 1941   12 OTU

Sergeant D.A. McKenzie was killed by the airscrew of a Wellington.

Donald Alexander McKenzie, RAFVR, s/n 989284, age 19, son of Donald and Marion McKenzie of Stretford. Died on 21 February 1941 and is buried in Stretford Cemetery.

23 February 1941   PRU

Acting Flight Lieutenant F.M. Lockyer failed to return from a Spitfire high level sortie to the Belgium coast. The PRU daily operations sheet gives no other details.

Flight Lieutenant Lockyer, s/n 37193, in Spitfire R6598 of 1 PRU was captured and became a prisoner of war, number 470, at Stalag Luft III.

27 February 1941   RAF Station Benson

A single Ju 88 approached Benson from the south and flew across the aerodrome at approximately 250 feet, machine-gunning aircraft near the hangars and dropping four HE bombs estimated to be 450 kilos with three second delayed action fuses. These bombs fell in a stick approximately 150 yards from the hangars. Sergeant WOP E. Featherstone was killed in a Wellington aircraft, on the ground, which was destroyed by a bomb. Damage to other aircraft was as follows -

> Blenheim IV V5808 Repairable at Base
> Blenheim I K7143 Repairable at Base
> Spitfire I PR X4384 Repairable at Base
> Spitfire I P9385 Repairable at Base

The enemy aircraft had previously flown over the satellite at Mount Farm machine-gunning but dropping no bombs. Two machine-gun posts opened fire at Benson but it is believed the enemy aircraft was hit over the satellite station at Mount Farm.

Edwin Featherstone RAF, s/n 628378, age 19. Son of Edwin and Nellie Featherstone of Gorton, Manchester. Died on 27 February 1941 and is buried in Manchester Southern Cemetery.

28 February 1941   12 OTU

A Wellington aircraft, R1285, crashed at 1100 hours at Watlington. Sergeant E.F. Fry and Pilot Officer F.H.S. West, (attached from 142 Squadron) the sole occupants, were both killed. There was slight damage to property.

Edward Frank Fry DFM RAFVR, s/n 741738, age 26. Son of William and Eva Fry of Sidcup. Died on 28 February 1941 and is buried in Sittingbourne Cemetery, Kent.

Frederick Hornby Sutcliffe West RAFVR, s/n 66507, age 23, son of Edwin and Marjorie West of Wimbledon, Surrey. Died on 28 February 1941 and is buried in Benson (St Helen) Churchyard Extension.

12 March 1941   Mount Farm

Mount Farm was bombed at 2255 hours. Thirteen small HE bombs were dropped; one NCO was killed and three airmen slightly injured; there was no damage to any buildings.

The NCO who was killed is thought to have been Corporal Norman Grenville Jones, s/n 348270 who died on 12 March 1941 and is buried in Benson (St Helen) Churchyard Extension.

18 March 1941　　　　　　　　12 OTU

A Wellington aircraft of No. 12 OTU crashed at Watlington at 0058 hours while night flying. Pilot Officer T.M. Couper and Sergeant D. McLean were both killed; Sergeant Wanek was seriously injured.

Thomas Mackintosh Couper, RCAF, s/n J/3742, age 20, son of William and Jean Couper of Toronto, Ontario, Canada. Buried in Benson (St Helen) Churchyard Extension.

Donald McLean, RCAF, s/n R/66040, age 22, son of Donald and Beatrice McLean of Niagara Falls, Ontario, Canada. Buried in Benson (St Helen) Churchyard Extension.

19 March 1941　　　　　　　　RAF Station Benson

HRH Group Captain the Duke of Kent visited the station.

31 March 1941　　　　　　　　PRU

Pilot Officer J.K. Punshon failed to return from a sortie to the Rotterdam area. The PRU daily operations sheet gives no further details.

Jonathan Killingworth Punshon, s/n 42724, age 19, son of Hugh Punshon MVO and Victoria Punshon of Cobham, Surrey. Died on 31 March 1941 and is commemorated on the Runnymede Memorial.

7 April 1941　　　　　　　　RAF Station Benson

Wellington I L4342 arrived from Vickers Ltd at Blackpool.

10 April 1941　　　　　　　　PRU

Flying Officer W. Manifould and Flying Officer L. Loasby both failed to return from sorties in Spitfires to the Brest area. The PRU daily operations sheet gives no further details.

William Kenneth Manifould RAFVR, s/n 81658, son of William and Ethel Manifould of Wokingham, Berkshire. Died on 10 April 1941 and is commemorated on the Runnymede Memorial.

Laurence David Loasby RAF, s/n 36242, age 23, son of David and Olive Loasby of Greytown, Wellington, New Zealand. Died on 10 April 1941 and is commemorated on the Runnymede Memorial.

14 April 1941   PRU

Sergeant W. Morgan took photos of Genoa and Spezia and force landed in a field near to RAF Hawkinge after being in the air for 7 hours and 10 minutes with only 2 gallons of petrol left. This is the longest trip ever carried out by a Spitfire. On 16 April 1941 Sergeant Morgan was awarded the DFM.

14 April 1941   PRU

Blenheim IV V5736 with crew: pilot, Pilot Officer J.K. Flynn, observer, Pilot Officer W.C. Hall and air gunner, Sergeant R.A. Stephens, failed to return from a sortie to the Dutch Coast.

James Kevin Flynn, s/n 42462, age 26, son of Edward and Margaret Flynn, husband of Norah F. Flynn of Armagh, Northern Ireland. Died on 14 April 1941 and is buried in Flushing (Vlissingen) Northern Cemetery.

William Clifford Hall, RAFVR, s/n 78264, age 30, son of William and Barbara Hall of Ovington, Northumberland. Died on 14 April 1941 and is buried in Flushing (Vlissingen) Northern Cemetery.

Robert Arthur Stephens, s/n 551633, age 19, son of Edgar and Gladys Stephens of Carharrack, Cornwall. Died on 14 April 1941 and is buried in Flushing (Vlissingen) Northern Cemetery.

15 April 1941   PRU

'D' flight left for RAF Station Wick.
'B' flight returned from Wick to RAF Station Benson.

20 April 1941   RAF Station Benson

Flight Lieutenant L. Clark DFC, late of 'B' flight, visited PRU. He had flown a Boeing 17c (Flying Fortress) from Canada earlier in the week.

28 April 1941   PRU

Spitfire I N3241 crashed on landing at Benson. Neither the name of the pilot nor any other details were given.

30 April 1941   **PRU St Eval detachment**

Spitfire I N3117 crash landed at St Eval. PRU daily operations sheet gives no other details.

30 April 1941   **PRU**

Flying Officer S.H. Dowse, whilst on a sortie, was intercepted by a formation of four Me109s. He took evasive action by turning in over Germany and dived to 10,000 feet. He was in the air for 5 hours and force landed in a field near Ipswich through lack of fuel.

3 May 1941   **PRU**

Sergeant P.G. Rose in Spitfire I R6805 failed to return from a sortie over the Ruhr area.

Peter Garratt Rose, RAFVR, s/n 748692, age 25, son of John and Ida Rose of Burton-on-Trent. Died on 3 May 1941 and is buried in Soumagne Communal Cemetery, Belgium.

3 May 1941   **PRU**

Flying Officer W. Panton in Spitfire I PR X4495 failed to return from a sortie to Cambrai.

William Panton DFC, s/n 43150, age 27. Died on 3 May 1941 and is commemorated on the Runnymede Memorial.

10 May 1941   **PRU**

Sergeant P.A. Mills in Spitfire I P9552 failed to return from an operational sortie, PRU daily operations sheet gives no other details.

Peter Alan Mills, RAFVR, s/n 741481, age 23, son of Alan and Helen Mills of Cambridge. Died on 10 May 1941 and is commemorated on the Runnymede Memorial.

10 May 1941   **PRU St Eval detachment**

'C' Flight at St Eval was bombed during the night. Only one aircraft, Blenheim T2444, was seriously damaged, and there were no injuries to personnel.

Flying Officer Dowse. [See 30 April, 20 August and 10 September 1941]

St Eval. HRH the Duke of Kent talking to Flying Officer William Panton, third from the right. [See 3 May 1941]

25 May 1941 — PRU

Spitfire V X4335 reported crashed and Spitfire I R7070 reported missing. PRU daily operations sheet gives no other details.

25 May 1941 — PRU St Eval

Flying Officer R.W. Ayres DFC was reported missing from a sortie to Brest; a Blenheim aircraft from 'F' Flight carried out a search without success.

Robert William Ayres, s/n 40292, age 20, son of Frank and Lilian Ayres of Sutton Coldfield, Warwickshire. Died on 25 May 1941 and is commemorated on the Runnymede Memorial.

31 May 1941

The discovery of the month was of the *Bismarck* near Bergen by a Spitfire from the PRU unit at RAF Wick.

Camouflaging experiments were carried out during the month at Benson and it was found that a very pale pink colour was extremely successful.

2-8 June 1941 — PRU St Eval

During the above period 'C' Flight at St Eval located the *Prinz Eugen*. This caused considerable excitement and the film was flown to Bomber Command the same evening.

7 June 1941 — RAF Station Benson

Two Martin Maryland I aircraft arrived today, S/Nos. AR730 and AR734. They had flown from the Burtonwood Repair Depot at Warrington, Lancashire.

9 June 1941 — PRU RAF Wick

Pilot Officer I.B. Cooper took-off in Spitfire I PR X4496 on a sortie to the Norwegian coast and failed to return. Later, on 1 September 1941, it was established that Pilot Officer Cooper was killed in action as his body, upon which was his cheque book, was washed ashore at Gothenburg, Sweden.

Ivan Brian Cooper, RAFVR, s/n 61289, age 20, son of Brian and Ruth Cooper of Merrivale, Natal, South Africa. Died on 9 June 1941 and is buried in Ockero Churchyard, Sweden.

Spitfire in pale pink camouflage. [See 31 May 1941]

The German heavy cruiser *Prinz Eugen*. [See 2-8 June 1941] This photo was taken in November 1942 by PRU when the ship was in dock in Gdynia.

16 June 1941
No. 1 PRU was today formed at RAF Station Benson.

18 June 1941   **RAF Station Benson**
The Maryland Flight is to be known as 'G' Flight.

19 June 1941   **12 OTU**
There was a fatal accident involving a Wellington, while night flying. The crew, all trainees, were killed. Crew names as follows:
    Sergeant H. Ursell (Pilot)
    Sergeant H.W. Parry, H.W.
    Sergeant K.T. Mitchell, K.T. (WOP/AG)
    Sergeant L.O. Hodnett, (WOP/AG)

Howard Ursell, RAFVR, s/n 1256526, age 19, son of Ernest and Ethel Ursell of Hampton. Middlesex. Died on 19 June 1941 and is buried in Brookwood Military Cemetery, Surrey.

Herbert William Parry, RAFVR, s/n 1181625, age 19, son of Herbert and Gertrude Parry of Isleworth, Middlesex. Died on 19 June 1941 and is buried in Benson (St Helen) Churchyard Extension.

Kenneth Turner Mitchell, s/n 1002064, age 20, son of James and Susan Mitchell of Laurieston, Falkirk. Died on 19 June 1941 and is buried in Muiravonside Cemetery.

Leslie Owen Hodnett, RAFVR, s/n 1158544, age 19, son of William and Alice Hodnett of Stourbridge. Died on 19 June 1941 and is buried in Wollaston (St James) Churchyard.

23 June 1941   **RAF Station Benson**
 A Maryland with crew members Flying Officer Peters DFC
                                Sergeant Palmer
                                Sergeant Chadwick
left Benson at 0800 hours and, after briefing at RAF Kemble, it refuelled at St Eval. The aircraft arrived safely at Gibraltar at 1838 hours on 24 June 1941. Its ETA was 1835 hours.
 The aircraft made its first sortie on 25 June 1941.

29 June 1941   **RAF Station Benson**

The chapel, which forms part of the gymnasium building, was dedicated by the Right Reverend the Bishop of Dorchester.

29 June 1941   **RAF Station Benson**

Squadron Leader D.A.H. Robson, MO of No. 1 PRU and later MO of the Station was killed in a Flying Fortress while flying at 17,000 feet over Catterick. There was only one survivor out of seven personnel aboard.

David Alan Hope Robson, s/n 23394, age 32, son of Charles and Joan Hope Robson, husband of Rosemary Hope Robson of Wallington, Surrey. Buried Catterick Cemetery. [The Commonwealth War Graves Commission gives the date of death as 22 June 1941.]

30 June 1941   **PRU**

Pilot Officer S. Bowes in Spitfire I K9787 took-off at 1445 hours for Le Havre but failed to return.

Samuel Bowes, s/n 44672, age 25, son of Samuel and Daisy Bowes of Thornton Heath, Surrey. Died on 30 June 1941 and is commemorated on the Runnymede Memorial.

2 July 1941   **RAF Station Benson**

The second Maryland left for Gibraltar today.

8 July 1941   **RAF St Eval**

Spitfire I N3111 crashed at St Eval. No further details given.

10 July 1941   **12 OTU**

At 0900 hours the advance party of No. 12 OTU left for Chipping Warden.

13 July 1941   **No. 1 PRU**

The first Mosquito I W4051 arrived by air from RAF Boscombe Down. It later returned to de Havilland at Hatfield.

15 July 1941   **No. 1 PRU**

'E' Flight left for RAF Wick and 'D' Flight returned to Benson.

The chapel at RAF Benson. [See 29 June 1941]

Flying Officer Michael Suckling. [See 21 July 1941]

21 July 1941   No. 1 PRU

No. 3 PRU arrived from RAF Oakington to become part of this unit.

No. 3 PRU aircraft complement as follows -

    Spitfire I R6903
    Spitfire V X4385
    Spitfire V X4494
    Spitfire V X4493
    Spitfire V X4498
    Spitfire V X4383
    Spitfire I R6902

21 July 1941   No. 1 PRU

Flying Officer M.F. Suckling in Spitfire I R6903 failed to return from an operational sortie to La Pallice.

Michael Frank Suckling, s/n 42907, age 21. Died on 21 July 1941 and is commemorated on the Runnymede Memorial.

23 July 1941   Mount Farm

The satellite at Mount Farm was today taken over by No. 15 OTU from RAF Station Harwell.

25 July 1941   RAF Station Benson

The Commander-in-Chief Air Chief Marshal Sir Philip Joubert de la Forte KCB CMG DSO visited the station.

25 July 1941   RAF Station St Eval

Flight Lieutenant K.F. Arnold was killed while ferrying an aircraft. No other details known.

Keith Fergus Arnold, s/n 39012, age 30, son of Harry and Eva Arnold of Saskatoon, Saskatchewan, Canada. Died on 25 July 1941 and is buried in St Eval Churchyard.

28 July 1941   No. 1 PRU

Pilot Officer J.K. Charles-Jones is reported missing from an operational sortie to Norway. PRU daily operations sheet gives no other details.

John Kenneth Charles-Jones, s/n 44661, age 23, son of Ernest and Edith Charles-Jones of Penhow, Monmouthshire. Died on 27/28 July 1941 and is commemorated on the Runnymede Memorial.

10 August 1941   No. 1 PRU
Mosquito I W4051 arrived back from de Havilland at Hatfield.

15 August 1941   No. 1 PRU
No. 1 PRU came under No. 16 Group for administration as from today, thus transferring from Bomber Command to Coastal Command.

20 August 1941   No. 1 PRU
Flying Officer S.H. Dowse in Spitfire V X4497 failed to return from an operational sortie to Brest. *See* 10 September 1941.

20 August 1941   No. 1 PRU
Flying Officer C.A.S. Greenhill DFC in Spitfire V X4491 failed to return from an operational sortie to Brest. *See* 1 September 1941.

26 August 1941   RAF Station Benson
Curtiss Tomahawk 2596M was dispatched by road today to No. 1 School of Technical Training at RAF Halton.

26 August 1941   No.1 PRU
Spitfire V X4501 crashed and was written off. PRU daily operations sheet gives no other details.

27 August 1941   RAF Station Benson
Group Captain J. Bussey arrived to take over command of the station.

28 August 1941   No. 1 PRU
Flying Officer P. Harding in Spitfire V X4493 failed to return from an operational sortie to Kiel. Later it was reported that the pilot was a POW.

Peter Harding s/n 73046 of 1 PRU was captured after the engine of his aircraft stopped over Wilhelmshaven and he had to bale out. He became a prisoner of war, number 3748, at Stalag Luft III from where he was released in May 1945.

Flying Officer Greenhill.
[See 20 August & 1 September 1941]

Flying Officer Blair.
[See 1 September 1941]

Flying Officer Harding, left, and friends taking a well-earned rest.
[See 28 August 1941]

1941

29 August 1941 **RAF Station Benson**
Avro Anson N9908 arrived by air from 48 Squadron at Stornaway.

1 September 1941 **1416 Flight**
No. 1416 Flight have now arrived at Benson equipped with Spitfires, Blenheims and a Lysander and will be operating from here. Later, on 17 September 1941, this unit became 140 Squadron.

1 September 1941 **No. 1 PRU**
Flying Officer C.C. Blair in Spitfire V X4500 failed to return from an operational sortie to Norway.

Colin Campbell Blair, RAFVR, s/n77781, age 26, son of the Revd Duncan Blair MC DD and Ada Blair of Bearsden, Dunbartonshire, Scotland. Died on 1 September 1941 and is commemorated on the Runnymede Memorial.

1 September 1941 **No. 1 PRU**
News has been received that Flying Officer C.A.S. Greenhill who failed to return from a sortie to Brest on 20 August is now a prisoner of war.

Flying Officer Greenhill, s/n 40906, in Spitfire X4491 of 1 PRU became prisoner of war, number 3721 at Stalag Luft III.

10 September 1941 **PRU**
Pilot Officer G.N. Busbridge took-off in Spitfire V R7039 on a recce of the Franco-Spanish border, but failed to return.

George Norcott Busbridge, s/n 87428, age 26, son of George and Dorothy Busbridge of Harrietsham, Kent. Died on 10 September 1941 and is commemorated on the Runnymede Memorial.

10 September 1941 **No. 1 PRU**
Information has been received that Flying Officer S.H. Dowse who failed to return from a sortie on 20 August is now a prisoner of war and that he has injuries to his leg.

Flying Officer Dowse, s/n 86685, in a Spitfire of 1 PRU was captured and became a prisoner of war, number 39320, at Stalag Luft III.

13 September 1941 — RAF Station Benson

Sir Archibald Sinclair KT CMG MP visited the station. He was taken for 15 minute flight in a Mosquito and was very impressed.

15 September 1941 — No.1 PRU

Spitfire IA X4786 crashed on landing, no other details given.

16 September 1941 — PRU St Eval

Flight Lieutenant Lofts DFC in Spitfire V X4384 took-off at 1515 hours on a sortie to Lorient and Nantes but crashed on returning to base at 1555 hours. The pilot survived the crash.

20 September 1941 — No. 1 PRU

The Air Ministry Film Production Unit is now based with No. 1 PRU. Flight Sergeant Parrott has flown film producers and camera men over a large part of the North Sea getting shots of what will eventually be Coastal Command's equivalent of *Target for Tonight*.

22 September 1941 — RAF Station Benson

Two Russian officers, a colonel and a major, visited the station. The colonel was a test pilot and has flown in many types of operational aircraft. He was flown in a Mosquito.

22 September 1941 — No. 1 PRU

Aircraft losses for this day. PRU daily operational sheet gives no other details.

From Benson	Spitfire V X4385
	Spitfire V X4333
From Wick	Spitfire I R7037

22 September 1941 — No. 1 PRU

Flight Lieutenant P. Tomlinson in Spitfire V X4385 failed to return from an operational sortie to Hamburg. PRU daily operations sheet gives no other details.

Flight Lieutenant P. Tomlinson, s/n 39154, in Spitfire X4385 of 1 PRU, was captured and became a prisoner of war, number 3805, at Stalag Luft III.

A BRIEF REPORT ON THE INTRODUCTION OF MOSQUITO AIRCRAFT TO BENSON

On the afternoon of 13 July 1941, eight months after the maiden flight of prototype W4050, W4051 arrived at Benson from Boscombe Down; W4054 arrived on 22 July 1941 and W4055 on 7 August 1941. By 13 September 1941 Benson had five PR Is and the sixth had flown. Operations by Mosquitos from Benson began with W4055 on 17 September 1941 to Brest and the Spanish/French border. By the end of February 1942 RAF Station Benson had flown no less than 88 PR sorties and lost one Mosquito. The first Mosquito to fly with pressure cabins was MP469 on 8 August 1942; this aircraft was a Mosquito XV, a special high altitude prototype. The very first prototype Mosquito, W4050, is now preserved back at its birthplace, Salisbury Hall, where it is available for public inspection.

Sir Archibald Sinclair prepares to take his first flight in a Mosquito.
[See 13 September 1941]

1 PRU 'B' Flight ground crew with their first Mosquito.

23 September 1941   **No. 1 PRU**

Mosquito 1 W4059 crashed on landing, no further details given.

26 September 1941   **RAF Station Benson**

The Chief of Air Staff Air Chief Marshal Sir Charles Portal KCB DSO MC visited the station.

30 September 1941   **No. 1 PRU**

Flying Officer J.F. Swift DFC in Spitfire V R7043 failed to return from an operational sortie to Kiel.

James Frederick Swift DFC, s/n 41080, age 24, son of George and Caroline Swift of Invercargill, Southland, New Zealand. Died on 30 September 1941 and is buried in Sage War Cemetery, Germany.

5 October 1941   **RAF Station Benson**

Professor R.V. Jones visited the station.

5 October 1941   **No. 1 PRU**

Squadron Leader R.F. Clarke of No. 1 PRU demonstrated the Mosquito before their Majesties The King and Queen at Watton. A mock fight with a Spitfire was arranged. The Spitfire was flown by Wing Commander Tuttle OBE DFC. The demonstration was staged to show the Mosquito's possibilities.

5 October 1941   **No. 1 PRU**

Flying Officer A.H.W. Ball flying in a Spitfire V R7033 at 23,000 feet over Bishops Stortford flew into a thunderstorm which made the aircraft unmanageable. The pilot was thrown out but landed safely by parachute.

7 October 1941   **No. 1 PRU**

Sergeant Jones in Spitfire V AA785 took-off at 1125 hours on a sortie to Copenhagen but crashed on returning to base at 1630 hours. The pilot survived the crash.

11 October 1941   **RAF Station Benson**

Flying Officer R.F. Leavitt DFC is reported missing, flying a Hudson from Canada.

Robert Frederick Leavitt DFC, s/n 42238, of 1 PRU, age 25, son of Sherman and Clara Leavitt of Regina, Saskatchewan, Canada. Commemorated on the Runnymede Memorial. [According to the Commonwealth War Graves Commission the date of Flying Officer Leavitt's death is 21 September 1941 which is likely to be the date he left Canada for the trans-Atlantic flight.]

19 October 1941   No. 1 PRU
Squadron Leader R.F. Clarke flew in a record time of 1 hour 32 minutes from Wick to Benson in a Mosquito.

24 October 1941   RAF Station Benson
Ansons AX180 and AX228 arrived from A.V. Roe at Woodford.

24 October 1941   No. 1 PRU
Spitfire IA R7147 crashed; later it was dispatched to No. 1 CRU at Cowley for repair.

24 October 1941   No. 1 PRU
Wing Commander Stratton posted to No. 1 PRU to take over from Wing Commander Tuttle. He took over the station command on 28 October 1941.

24 October 1941   RAF Station Benson
The following aircraft arrived
  Anson AX229 from Chester
  Anson W2635 from Yeadon
  Anson W2637 from Yeadon

28 October 1941   No. 1 PRU
Spitfire VA X4672 crashed. *See* 30 October 1941.

28 October 1941   RAF Station Benson
Wing Commander G.W. Tuttle OBE, DFC posted to RAF Station Tiree wef 7 November 1941.

29 October 1941   No. 1 PRU
Pilot Officer E.R. Hamer in Spitfire V AA801 on a camera test, crashed near Watchfield and was killed. *See* 5 November 1941.

Ernest Raymond Hamer, RAFVR, s/n 100630, age 20, son of Ernest and Mary Hamer of Darlington. Buried in Darlington West Cemetery.

Wing Commander Geoffrey W. Tuttle OBE DFC. [See 5 and 24 October 1941]

Squadron Leader Alistair L. Taylor DFC. [See 4 December 1941]

30 October 1941   No. 1 PRU
Spitfire VA X4672, previously reported crashed, was today dispatched to the Heston Aircraft Company for repair.

1-4 November 1941   140 Squadron
An Armament Training camp was held at Weston Zoyland. An extensive Air Firing programme was carried out with
- 3 Spitfires
- 3 Blenheims
- 3 Lysanders

5 November 1941   No. 1 PRU
Crash as reported on 29 October 1941 Spitfire V AA801 was written off.

6 November 1941   No. 1 PRU
Spitfire V AA783 crashed on landing, no further details given.

15 November 1941   RAF Station Benson
Blenheims IV Z5806 and Z5807 are written off and dispatched to Cunliffe Owen at Southampton.

21 November 1941   No. 140 Squadron
Three Spitfires went to Old Sarum to give a demonstration of Air Photography to officers of No. 5 Corps; sorties were successful.

24 November 1941   No. 140 Squadron
Flying Officer N.R. Peel in Spitfire R6610 failed to return from an operational sortie to Grandcamp and the Caen area.

Nicholas Richard Peel, s/n 42431, age 22, son of the Revd Harold Peel MA and Mary Peel of Woodborough Rectory, Wiltshire. Died on 24 November 1941 and is buried in Grandcamp-les-Bains Churchyard, France.

25 November 1941   RAF Station Benson
Blenheim IV R6080 was written off, and dispatched to No. 30 MU at Sealand.

27 November 1941   RAF Station Benson

Maryland I arrived from No. 43 Group, and is now written off charge.

2 December 1941   PRU

Sergeant L. Briggs took-off at 1100 hours in Spitfire V R7040 to Brest, St Nazaire, and La Pallice, but failed to return.

Leonard Briggs, RAFVR, s/n 758051, age 21, son of Thomas and Mary Briggs of Blackpool, Lancashire. Died on 2 December 1941 and is commemorated on the Runnymede Memorial.

4 December 1941   No. 1 PRU Wick

Squadron Leader A.L. Taylor DFC (ace pilot of the unit) and Sergeant S.E. Horsfall in Mosquito PR I W4055 – aircraft known to the crews as Benedictine – failed to return from the Trondheim/Bergen area and is believed to have been shot down by enemy gunfire. The aircraft took-off from RAF Station Wick at 1015 hours and is the first Mosquito of this type to be lost.

Alistair Lennox Taylor, s/n 39448, age 25, son of Alfred and Marie Taylor of Alderton, Gloucestershire. Died on 4 December 1941 and is commemorated on the Runnymede Memorial.

Sidney Edward Horsfall, RAFVR, s/n 921014, age 27, son of Herbert and Nellie Horsfall, husband of Stella Horsfall of Bournemouth, Hampshire. Died on 4 December 1941 and is commemorated on the Runnymede Memorial.

9 December 1941   1 PRU

Flying Officer J.M.H. Sargent in Spitfire N3117 took-off at 1105 on a sortie to Berck-sur-Mer, Pas de Calais but failed to return.

John Michael Hewlett Sargent, formerly 2nd Lieutenant, Royal Tank Regiment, s/n 43553, age 24, son of the Reverend Laurens Sargent and Mrs Ethel Sargent of St Peter-in-Thanet, Kent. Died on 9 December 1941 and is commemorated on the Runnymede Memorial.

16 December 1941   No. 140 Squadron

Flying Officer C.A.P. Christie crashed and was killed near Corfe Castle whilst carrying out a high level sortie in Spitfire R7142.

Charles Alexander Peter Christie, formerly 2nd Lieutenant, Royal Inniskilling Fusiliers, s/n 43094, age 22, son of Mrs M.H.E. Christie of Chelsea, London. Buried in Hoddesdon Cemetery, Hertfordshire.

December 1941

Extremely bad weather during this month badly curtailed operations.

1942

11 January 1942 **No. 1 PRU**
Mosquito 1 W4062
Mosquito 1 W4063
were both dispatched today to No. 44 Group.

25 January 1942 **No. 1 PRU**
Flying Officer A.P.L. Barber in Spitfire V AA813 failed to return on operations flight returning from Gibraltar.

Anthony Perrinott Lysberg Barber, s/n 45056 baled out of his aircraft near to Mont St Michel and became prisoner of war number 1411 at Stalag Luft III.

After the war he became a Conservative MP serving in a number of senior posts before becoming Chancellor of the Exchequer in 1970. In 1974, as Lord Barber of Wentbridge, he went to the House of Lords.

26 January 1942 **No. 1 PRU**
Flying Officer P.W. Herbert died of injuries received on crashing on 24 January 1942.

Philip Wynne Herbert, RAFVR, s/n 82676, age 26, son of Air Commodore Philip Lee William Herbert and Gwendolin Hughes Herbert of Theale. His brothers Richard V. and Gerald B. Herbert also died on service. Flying Officer Herbert is buried in Theale (Holy Trinity) Churchyard.

The long-range fuel tanks that were fitted to Mosquito I W4062 and Mosquito I W4063 of I PRU.

Pilot Officer A. Gunn who became a prisoner of war after failing to return from a sortie. [See 5 March 1942]

1942

The weather was again bad during the month of January and on the 18th, 19th and 20th there was no flying. On the 23 January 1942 Benson aerodrome was unserviceable and operations were diverted to Mount Farm.

6 February 1942   RAF Station Benson
Avro Anson AX229 was written off charge.

23 February 1942   No. 1 PRU
Flight Lieutenant E.J. Durston took-off at 0758 hours on a low level sortie to Katwijk in Holland in Spitfire V AA787 but failed to return.

Eric John Durston, s/n 42051, age 22, son of John and Olivia Durston of Wellington, Somerset. Died on 23 February 1942 and is buried in Bergen General Cemetery, Holland.

February   140 Squadron
During February, despite adverse weather conditions, the Squadron carried out numerous sorties, especially to the Cherbourg, Barfleur, Dieppe and Dunkirk areas.

1 March 1942   No. 1 PRU
Spitfire V AB300 was dispatched to No. 2 PRU in the Middle East.

5 March 1942   No. 1 PRU
Pilot Officer A. Gunn took-off at 0807 hours in Spitfire V AA810 on an operational sortie to Trondheim, but failed to return.

Prisoner of War records show this officer as Flying Officer A.D.M. Gunn, s/n 60340, of 1 PRU. No details of the prison camp are available.

13 March 1942   No. 1 PRU
Pilot Officer A. Macdonald in Spitfire V AA783 took-off at 1140 hours on operations to Wilhelmshaven and Emden but failed to return.

Prisoner of War records show this officer as Flight Lieutenant A.T. McDonald, s/n 115420, of 1 PRU. He was captured and became a prisoner of war, number 16, at Stalag Luft III.

17 March 1942   140 Squadron

Flying Officer T. Nicholson in Spitfire X4907 took-off at 1300 hours for the Le Touquet area. On his return, in conditions of very low cloud and poor visibility, he crashed into the side of Trundle Hill near Goodwood and was killed.

Tom Nicholson, s/n 77948, age 34, son of Thomas and Mary Nicholson of Wrea Green. Died on 17 March 1942 and is buried in Ribby-with-Wrea (St Nicholas) Churchyard.

18 March 1942   No. 1 PRU Wick

Flight Sergeant R.D.C. Tomlinson in Spitfire V R7035 took-off at 1000 hours on an operational sortie to Bergen but failed to return.

Robert Duncan Campbell Tomlinson, s/n 905231, age 30, son of Reginald and Ellen Tomlinson of Pietermaritzburg, Natal, South Africa. Died on 18 March 1942 and is commemorated on the Runnymede Memorial.

27 March 1942   No. 1 PRU

Flight Lieutenant A.R. Densham in Spitfire VA AR245 took-off at 1000 hours on an operational sortie to Le Havre but failed to return.

Arthur Roy Densham, s/n 41157, age 29, son of Arthur and Eleanor Densham of Purley, Surrey. Died on 27 March 1942 and is commemorated on the Runnymede Memorial.

29 March 1942   RAF Station Benson

Avro Anson DJ182 arrived from A.V. Roe at Yeadon.

2 April 1942   No. 1 PRU

Pilot Officer I. Hutcheson and Pilot Officer B.K. Allen in Mosquito W4056 took-off on an operational sortie to Trondheim but failed to return.

Prisoner of War records show Pilot Officer Hutcheson as Flight Lieutenant I. Hutchinson, s/n 102960, of 1 PRU. All other details are the same as above. He was captured and became a prisoner of war, number 163, at Stalag Luft III.

Pilot Officer B.K. Allen, s/n 119514, of 1 PRU was also captured and became a prisoner of war, number 136, at Stalag Luft III.

2 April 1942   No. 1 PRU Wick

Flight Sergeant M.A. Jones in Spitfire V AA797 failed to return from an operational sortie to Trondheim.

Mervyn Anthony Jones, RAFVR, s/n 748630, age 23, son of Herbert and Anne Jones of Carmarthen. Rode the winner of the Grand National Steeplechase, 1940. Died on 2 April 1942 and is commemorated on the Runnymede Memorial.

10 April 1942   No. 1 PRU St Eval

Flying Officer J.B. Ayer in Spitfire PR I R7056 took-off at 0945 hours on an operational sortie to St Malo but failed to return.

John Butler Ayer, RAFVR, s/n 83702, died on 10 April 1942 and is commemorated on the Runnymede Memorial.

10 April 1942   No. 1 PRU Wick

Flying Officer P.G.C. Gimson in Spitfire PR IV AB307 took-off at 1011 hours on an operational sortie to Trondheim but failed to return.

Peter Geoffrey Charles Gimson, RAFVR, s/n 60764, age 23, son of Geoffrey and Mary Gimson of Leicester. Died on 10 April 1942 and is buried in Trondheim (Stavne) Cemetery, Norway.

12 April 1942   No. 1 PRU

Flying Officer E.W.R. Fortt in Spitfire PR IV AA798 crashed in England while on a sortie to the Rotterdam area. The pilot was killed. Later the aircraft was sent to No. 43 Group but on 16 April 1942 it was written off.

Edward William Ronald Fortt, RCAF, s/n C/1616, age 21, son of Colonel Ronald L. and Mrs Fortt of Victoria, British Columbia, Canada. Died on 12 April 1942 and is buried in Saffron Walden Cemetery.

Flying Officer, later Flight Lieutenant, Arthur Densham who failed to return from an operation to photograph Le Havre. [See 27 March 1942]

Pilot Officer F.J. Blackwood BEM. After escaping unhurt from the crash landing on 22 April he was lost on a sortie to the Cherbourg peninsula. [See 2 June 1942]

1942

12 April 1942 **No. 1 PRU**

Warrant Officer Ball in Spitfire 1 R7036 took-off at 1415 hours on a sortie to Bremerhaven, Wilhelmshaven, Bremen and Groningen but failed to return.

Believed to be Melville Henry Ball (Pilot Officer) RAFVR, s/n 117461, age 21, son of Sydney and Matilde Ball of Rosario, Sante Fe Argentina. Buried Montrose (Sleepyhillock) Cemetery, Scotland.

14 April 1942 **No. 1 PRU**

Spitfire V BP907 dispatched to No. 2 PRU now missing and written off charge.

17 April 1942 **140 Squadron**

Flying Officer Muspratt in Spitfire R7028 took-off at 0855 hours on a high level sortie to Cherbourg. On his return at 1015 hours he was forced to make a belly landing at base, as the undercarriage had jammed up.

18 April 1942 **No. 1 PRU St Eval**

Sergeant V.E.M. Henry in Spitfire V AB119 took-off at 1003 hours on a sortie to St Malo but failed to return.

Valentine Ernest Michael Henry, RAAF, s/n 404245, age 26, son of Michael and Evangeline Henry of Palmwoods, Queensland, Australia. Died on 18 April 1942 and is buried in Perros-Guirec Communal Cemetery, France.

22 April 1942 **No. 1 PRU**

Flight Sergeant C.M.T. Rogers in Spitfire V AB425 took-off on an operational sortie to the Emden area but failed to return.

Charles Matthew Thomas Rogers, RAFVR, s/n 912386, age 22, son of Charles and Mary Rogers of Wembley, Middlesex. Died on 22 April 1942 and is commemorated on the Runnymede Memorial.

22 April 1942 **140 Squadron**

Pilot Officer F.J. Blackwood BEM in Spitfire X4492 took-off on a high level sortie to Cherbourg. The pilot found the contrail layer when at 25, 300 feet, so climbed above it, reaching the top at 37,000 feet. As he was turning on to his run he saw white smoke coming out of his starboard exhaust so he turned for home. The engine seized up and he glided down and crash landed in a field near to the unserviceable Sandown aerodrome on the Isle of Wight. The aircraft was considerably damaged, but the pilot escaped unhurt.

24 April 1942   140 Squadron

Pilot Officer C.B. Barber took-off on a sortie to the Pas de Calais in Spitfire X4784 but failed to return.

Charles Bertram Barber, RAFVR, s/n 47734, age 22, son of George and Edith Barber of Armthorpe, Yorkshire. Died on 24 April 1942 and is buried in Finningley (Holy Trinity & St Oswald) Churchyard Extension. For 44 years after failing to return from his last sortie, Pilot Officer Barber's whereabouts were unknown until, on 30 August 1986, his body was found, along with his aircraft, by the Tangmere Aviation Society, in a field by the River Brede near Rye in Sussex. He is, therefore, also commemorated on the Runnymede Memorial. He was laid to rest on 15 October 1986.

25 April 1942   No. 1 PRU

Pilot Officer I.D. Bourne in Spitfire V AA795 took-off at 1000 hours on a sortie to the Amiens area but failed to return.

Pilot Officer I.D. Bourne, s/n 108164, was captured and became prisoner of war number 192 at Stalag Luft III.

25 April 1942   No. 1 PRU

Wing Commander J.A.C. Stratton, Officer Commanding, was posted to RAF Station Talbenny as Station Commander. Squadron Leader S. Ring DFC took over this unit.

1 May 1942   140 Squadron

The unit received a new establishment to include 23 officers and 261 other ranks. The aircraft number was increased to include the two Spitfire IA training aircraft and the Tiger Moth, making a total of six Spitfires 'G' type, two 'F' type and two IA type. Also six Blenheim IVs and one Tiger Moth.

4 May 1942   **140 Squadron**

'A' and 'B' flights moved to Mount Farm to continue operations while the concrete runways were being completed at Benson. The movement was carried out smoothly and operations continued throughout the move. The movement affected one officer and 93 airmen who are to be administered by the Squadron HQ at Benson.

10 May 1942   **PRU Wick**

Flying Officer F.I. Malcolm in Spitfire V AB127 took-off at 0503 hours for a sortie to Trondheim but failed to return.

Frederick Ian Malcolm, s/n 43106, age 25, son of Frederick J. and Nancy Malcolm. Died on 10 May 1942 and is buried in Trondheim (Stavne) Cemetery, Norway.

20 May 1942   **140 Squadron**

HQ flight moved from Benson to Mount Farm to join 'A' and 'B' flights who were already operating from there. The move affected 18 officers and 49 other ranks. They were moved and operating within 24 hours of the receipt of the order to move. Maintenance Flight and part of the Photographic Section remained at Benson owing to the restricted facilities at Mount Farm and are to be considered a detached flight for all purposes. All administration for the Squadron will be effected from RAF Station at Mount Farm.

Wing Commander E.C. Le Mesurier DSO DFC assumes command of all RAF personnel of RAF Station Benson situated at Mount Farm and is granted powers of Subordinate Commander under KR and ACI paragraph 1141.

20 May 1942   **No. 1 PRU St Eval**

Sergeant A.A. Miller in Spitfire V AB129 took-off at 1002 hours on a sortie to the Bordeaux area but failed to return.

Albert Andrew Miller, RCAF, s/n R/62889, age 23, son of Thomas and Bessie Miller of Campbellton, New Brunswick, Canada. Died on 20 May 1942 and is commemorated on the Runnymede Memorial.

19-31 May 1942　　　　　　　**No.1 PRU Detachment at Gibraltar**

Maryland AR744 with crew of Pilot Officer R.L.C. Blyth, Flight Lieutenant E. Leatham and Sergeant R. Steele carried out nine recces from the RAF Station at Gibraltar.

2 June 1942　　　　　　　　**140 Squadron**

Pilot Officer F.J. Blackwood BEM in Spitfire X4502 took-off at 1120 hours for the Cherbourg peninsula but failed to return. An intercepted German R/T message claimed a British fighter was shot down four miles west of Alderney at a time coinciding with Pilot Officer Blackwood's sortie.

Francis John Blackwood, s/n 46821, age 28, son of Francis and Frances Blackwood of New Zealand, husband of Brenda Blackwood of Pedmore, Worcestershire. Died on 2 June 1942 and is commemorated on the Runnymede Memorial.

2 June 1942　　　　　　　　**140 Squadron**

Flying Officer C.K. Parkes in Spitfire AR234 took-off at 1700 hours on a sortie to St Valerie, Limat and Le Havre areas but failed to return.

Cranmer Kenneth Parkes, s/n 45326, age 22, son of Cranmer and Winifred Parkes of Alsager, Cheshire. Died on 2 June 1942 and is commemorated on the Runnymede Memorial.

3 June 1942　　　　　　　　**No. 1 PRU**

Sergeant J.C. McPherson in Spitfire V R7037 took-off at 1030 hours on a sortie to the Cherbourg and Le Havre areas but failed to return.

Joseph Campbell McPherson, RCAF, s/n R/85460, age 28, son of M. McPherson and Jessie Campbell McPherson of Wawota, Saskatchewan, Canada. Died on 3 June 1942 and is buried in Cherbourg Old Communal Cemetery, France.

16 June 1942　　　　　　　　**RAF Station Benson**

Wellington IV Z1417 arrived today from 44 MU at Prestwick.

17 June 1942　　　　　　　　**RAF Station Benson**

Wellington IV Z1418 arrived today from 44 MU at Prestwick.

19 June 1942   RAF Station Benson

Miles Master III W8786 was dispatched to No. 8 OTU at Fraserburgh.

5 July 1942   140 Squadron

Squadron Leader Webb DFC led four Spitfires and two Blenheims in formations over Windsor Castle on the occasion of a march past by the ATC. The AOC.-in-C. Sir Arthur S. Barratt KCB CMG MC took the salute.

12 July 1942   No. 1 PRU

Flight Lieutenant V.A. Ricketts DFC and Flight Sergeant G.B. Lukhmanoff in Mosquito II W4089 took-off at 1348 hours on an operations sortie, No. C57, to Strasbourg and Ingolstadt but failed to return.

Victor Anthony Ricketts, RAFVR, s/n 77341, age 29, son of William and Annie Ricketts, husband of Dorothy Ricketts of Streatham, London. Died on 12 July 1942 and is buried in Calais Canadian War Cemetery, Leubringhen, France.

Listed by the Commonwealth War Graves Commission as a Pilot Officer, George Boris Lukhmanoff DFM, RAFVR, s/n127470, age 24, son of Boris and Valentina Lukhmanoff of San Francisco, California, USA, died on 12 July 1942 and is buried in Calais Canadian War Cemetery, Leubringhen, France.

18 July 1942   No. 1 PRU

Flight Lieutenant Lane in Spitfire V BP921 took-off at 1255 hours on sortie C83 but crashed in this country and was killed. The aircraft crashed near Duxford; it was later dispatched to No. 43 Group. [Unable to discover any more details about this accident or the burial place of Flight Lieutenant Lane.]

22 July 1942   140 Squadron

Pilot Officer C.D. Harris St John took-off in Spitfire BP922 at 0705 hours and flew at 29,000 feet en route for Paris. The pilot was listening out on the new VHF radio and reported excellent reception throughout. This was the first time on which R/T has been used during daylight sorties by No. 140 Squadron.

27 July 1942 — No. 1 PRU at Leuchars

Flying Officer P.C. Sayce and Sergeant G.T. Thornton in Mosquito I W4067 took-off on sortie No. N601 to Oslo and Kristiansand but failed to return.

Patrick Campbell Sayce, RAFVR, s/n 84331, age 22, son of Mr & Mrs C.N. Sayce of Dovercourt, Essex, husband of J.F. Sayce. Died on 27 July 1942 and is commemorated on the Runnymede Memorial.

George Thomas Thornton, RAFVR, s/n 994179. Died on 27 July 1942 and is commemorated on the Runnymede Memorial.

29 July 1942 — 140 Squadron

General Sir Bernard C.T. Paget KCB DSO MC Commander-in-Chief Home Forces accompanied by Air Marshal Sir Arthur Barratt KCB CMG MC visited this Squadron today and inspected representative types of aircraft i.e. Blenheim IV, night flying Spitfires 'G' and 'Y' types of the unit. They witnessed the briefing and interrogating of pilots. The C.-in-C. departed at 1100 hours.

30 July 1942 — No. 1 PRU Wick

Flying Officer J.L. Tully in Spitfire V AA800 took-off on operations sortie No. F156 to Bergen but failed to return.

John Leahy Tully, RAAF, s/n 404189, age 28, son of Francis and Ann Tully of Quilpie, Queensland, Australia. Died on 30 July 1942 and is commemorated on the Runnymede Memorial.

30 July 1942 — No. 1 PRU

Pilot Officer Larson in Spitfire V BR417 took-off at 1425 hours on sortie No. C129 but crash landed at Ford. The aircraft was later dispatched to No. 43 Group.

30 July 1942 — No. 1 PRU

Flight Lieutenant H.M. Jones in Spitfire V AB301 took-off at 1530 hours on sortie No. C131 to Hamburg, Lübeck, Delmenhorst and Vegesack but failed to return.

Hayden Mortimer Jones, s/n 42233, age 26, son of Thomas and Violet Jones of Heronsgate, Chorleywood, Hertfordshire, husband of Shirley Jones of Princes Risborough, Aylesbury, Buckinghamshire. Died on 30 July 1942 and is commemorated on the Runnymede Memorial.

Pilot Officer C.D. Harris St John. [See 22 July 1942]

General Sir Bernard C.T. Paget KCB DSO MC, Commander-in-Chief Home Forces, in the pilot's seat, with Wing Commander E. Le Mesurier. [See 29 July 1942]

1 August 1942   No. 1 PRU

Warrant Officer W. Harrison in Spitfire AA781 took-off at 1540 hours on sortie No. C165 to Vegesack and Bremerhaven but failed to return.

Walter Harrison, RAFVR, s/n 740905, age 30, son of Walter and Grace H. Harrison of Sale, Cheshire, husband of F.M. Harrison. Died on 1 August 1942 and is commemorated on the Runnymede Memorial.

4 August 1942   No. 1 PRU

Pilot Officer Whitaker in Spitfire V AB314 took-off on sortie No. F159 to Trondheim but failed to return.

It is believed that Pilot Officer Whitaker became a prisoner of war although details of the camp in which he was incarcerated are not known.

11 August 1942   No. 1 PRU

Sergeant P. O'Connell in Spitfire IV AB120 took-off at 0933 hours on sortie No. C191 to Bremerhaven, Kiel, Bremen and the Wilhelmshaven area but failed to return.

Peter O'Connell, RAAF, s/n403761, age 20, son of Michael and Kathleen O'Connell of Lane Cove, NSW, Australia. Died on 11 August 1942 and is commemorated on the Runnymede Memorial.

17 August 1942   No. 1 PRU

Pilot Officer A.J.E.G. Cantillion in Spitfire PR IV AA814 took-off at 0950 hours on sortie C218 to Wilhelmshaven, Kiel, Emden and the Elbe area but failed to return.

Andre Joseph Emile Gregoire Cantillion, RAFVR, s/n 119856, age 22. A Belgian national, Pilot Officer Cantillion's body was returned to Belgium and he is remembered in The Maidenhead Register at the head office of the Commonwealth War Graves Commission.

17 August 1942   No. 1 PRU

Flight Sergeant Wright in Spitfire PR IV BP887 took-off at 0955 hours on sortie C220 to Vegesack, Hamburg and Bremerhaven but failed to return.

It is believed that Flight Sergeant Wright may have become a prisoner of war but no conclusive proof was found.

1942

21 August 1942 **No. 140 Squadron**

The operations record sheet for this day shows that seven Spitfires took-off at the same time, 0645 hours, on various sorties.

24 August 1942 **No. 1 PRU**

Flight Lieutenant Wooll and Sergeant Fielden in Mosquito IV DK310 took-off at 0925 hours on operations sortie No. C269 to Venice and Trieste, but failed to return. Information received later reported that the aircraft crash landed at Berne in Switzerland and the crew have been interned.

26 August 1942 **No. 140 Squadron**

Pilot Officer E.F. Lucarotti in Spitfire AB130 took-off at 1505 hours on a mission to Pontoise and Melun. While in cloud the instruments froze up one by one and the aircraft lost height from 23,000 feet to 3,000 feet. Being in cloud with the instruments still unserviceable, the pilot baled out near to East Grinstead and was slightly hurt when his parachute opened.

28 August 1942 **No. 1 PRU**

Sergeant F.C. Evans in Spitfire PR IV AB422 took-off on operational sortie No. C298 to Kassel but failed to return.

Frederick Charles Evans, s/n 521752, age 25, son of William and Sarah Evans, husband of Renee Evans of Cinderford, Gloucestershire. Died on 28 August 1942 and is buried in Tilburg (Gilzerbaan) General Cemetery, Holland.

28 August 1942 **No. 1 PRU**

Pilot Officer Devereux in Spitfire IV BP924 took-off at 1010 hours on operational sortie No. C299 to Cuxhaven, Bremerhaven and Kiel but failed to return.

It is believed that Pilot Officer Devereaux may have been a prisoner of war at Stalag Luft III but no positive proof could be found.

28 August 1942 **No. 1 PRU**

Flying Officer E.J. Harris in Spitfire IV AB317 took-off at 1030 hours on operations sortie No. C304 to Bingen, Lebach and Verdun but failed to return.

Eric John Harris, s/n 88224, age 30, son of Edward and Bertha Harris. Died on 28 August 1942 and is buried in Heverlee War Cemetery, Belgium.

1 September 1942   RAF Station Benson

Russian Detachment

At the beginning of September three Spitfires proceeded to Russia to carry out operations from a base there.

Russian Detachment Personnel.

Squadron Leader Wager to be Commanding Officer.
Pilots
    Flight Lieutenant Fairhurst
    Flying Officer Furniss
    Pilot Officer Walker
    Sergeant Hardman

Ground Staff
    Sergeant Greenwood
    Corporal Beer
    Corporal Ashton
    Leading Aircraftman Ashton
    Leading Aircraftman Cochrane
    Aircraftman Taylor

1 September 1942   No. 1 PRU Russian Detachment

Three Spitfires left Sumburgh and arrived at Afrikanda.

2 September 1942

Three Spitfires arrived at Vaenga.

7 September 1942   No. 1 PRU

Flight Lieutenant W.J. Scafe in Spitfire IV AA802 took-off at 0740 hours on operations sortie No. C 337 to Bremen but failed to return.

William John Scafe, s/n 43113. Died on 7 September 1942 and is buried in Sage War Cemetery, Germany.

9 September 1942
One Spitfire U/S from bomb splinters after enemy attack.

16 September 1942   No. 1 PRU
Pilot Officer Barraclough in Spitfire IV R7038 took-off at 0738 hours on operations sortie C391 to Bremen and Wilhelmshaven on D/A (damage assessment) but failed to return.

It is believed that Pilot Officer Barraclough may have been a prisoner of war at Stalag Luft III but no positive proof could be found.

19 September 1942
Sergeant Hardman arrived in PRU Spitfire at Vaenga after taking photographs of the Swedish/Finnish border on the way.

27 September 1942
Pilot Officer G.W. Walker reported missing from sorties ARC14 and ARC15.

Gavin William Walker, RAFVR, s/n 114418, age 24, son of Colonel J. Douglas and Mrs F. Walker of Borve, Isle of Harris. Died on 27 September 1942 and is buried in Tromso Cemetery, Norway. Pilot Officer Walker's brother Ian also died on service.

3 October 1942   140 Squadron
The Rt Hon Archibald Sinclair BT KT CMG MP Secretary of State for Air visited the Station (Mount Farm).

4 October 1942   140 Squadron
Lieutenant Colonel Elliott Roosevelt USAAF (son of President Franklin D. Roosevelt) accompanied by other USAAF officers, visited this Squadron and inspected various sections.

17 October 1942   No. 1 PRU Leuchars
Flying Officer D. Higson and Sergeant J.D. Hayes in Mosquito 1 W4058 took-off at 0930 hours on operations sortie No. 641 to mid Norway and Oslo but failed to return.

Donald Higson, s/n 44660. Died on 17 October 1942 and is buried in Oslo Western Civil Cemetery.

Pilot Officer E.F.
Lucarotti
[See 26 August 1942]

A visiting American B-17 – I Got Spurs – some of its crew and WAAFs from RAF Benson. [See 4 October 1942]

John Douglas Hayes, RAFVR, s/n 132171, age 25, son of William and Mary Hayes of Woodley, Reading, Berkshire. Died on 17 October 1942 and is buried in Oslo Western Civil Cemetery.

18 October 1942　　　　　　No. 1 PRU

No. 1 PRU ceased to exist after 18 October 1942 and the following aircraft were transferred to Squadrons from No. 1 PRU

To No. 540 Squadron

Mosquito I	W4051
Mosquito I	W4054
Mosquito I*	W4058
Mosquito I	W4059
Mosquito I	W4061
Mosquito II	DD615
Mosquito II	DD659
Mosquito IV	DK284
Mosquito IV	DK311
Mosquito IV	DK314
Mosquito IV	DK315
Mosquito IV	DK320

* This aircraft was reported as missing on the previous day, 17 October 1942.

No. 1 PRU aircraft transferred to 541 Squadron

Spitfire PR	IV	AA808	Merlin 45
Spitfire PR	IV	R7042	Merlin 45
Spitfire PR	IV	BR660	Merlin 46
Spitfire PR	IV	BP937	Merlin 46
Spitfire PR	IV	BR661	Merlin 46
Spitfire PR	IV	AA807	Merlin 45
Spitfire PR	IV	AB309	Merlin 45
Spitfire PR	IV	AB302	Merlin 45
Spitfire PR	IV	BP891	Merlin 46

Spitfire PR	IV	BP881	Merlin 45
Spitfire PR	IV	AA790	Merlin 45
Spitfire PR	IV	AB305	Merlin 45
Spitfire PR	IV	BP922	Merlin 46
Spitfire PR	IV	BP919	Merlin 46
Spitfire PR	VII	X4672	Merlin 45
Spitfire PR	VII	R7211	Merlin 45
Spitfire PR	VII	AR260	Merlin 45
Spitfire PR	VII	AR257	Merlin 45

No. 1 PRU aircraft transferred to 542 Squadron

Spitfire PR	IV	AB118	Merlin 45
Spitfire PR	IV	AB132	Merlin 45
Spitfire PR	IV	AB311	Merlin 45
Spitfire PR	IV	BP926	Merlin 46
Spitfire PR	IV	AB121	Merlin 45
Spitfire PR	IV	AA784	Merlin 45
Spitfire PR	IV	AA793	Merlin 45
Spitfire PR	IV	AB123	Merlin 45
Spitfire PR	IV	BP923	Merlin 46
Spitfire PR	IV	BR650	Merlin 46
Spitfire PR	VI	BP918	Merlin 46
Spitfire PR	VI	AB124	Merlin 45
Spitfire PR	VI	BP884	Merlin 46
Spitfire PR	VII	AR242	Merlin 45
Spitfire PR	VII	AR261	Merlin 45
Spitfire PR	VII	P9565	Merlin 45
Spitfire PR	IV	AB303	Merlin 45
Spitfire PR	IV	BP886	Merlin 46
Spitfire PR	IV	AB430	Merlin 45

No. 1 PRU aircraft transferred to 543 Squadron

Spitfire PR	IV	AA806	Merlin 45
Spitfire PR	IV	AA809	Merlin 45
Spitfire PR	IV	AB128	Merlin 45
Spitfire PR	IV	BR658	Merlin 46

1942

Spitfire PR	IV	BP889	Merlin 46
Spitfire PR	IV	AB306	Merlin 45
Spitfire PR	IV	AB424	Merlin 45
Spitfire PR	IV	BP917	Merlin 46
Spitfire PR	IV	AB427	Merlin 45
Spitfire PR	IV	AA803	Merlin 45
Spitfire PR	IV	BR420	Merlin 46
Spitfire PR	VII	X4786	Merlin 45
Spitfire PR	VII	AR235	Merlin 45
Spitfire PR	VII	R7139	Merlin 45
Spitfire PR	VII	N3111	Merlin 45

No. 1 PRU aircraft transferred to 544 Squadron

Spitfire PR	IV	BR666	Merlin 46
Wellington	IV	Z1417	
Wellington	IV	Z1418	
Anson		W2637	
Tiger Moth		N9305	
Anson		AX228	
Anson		DJ182	
Anson		W2635	
Maryland		AR744	

No. 1 PRU function now completed.

Introduction to 540 Squadron formation on 19 October 1942

Squadron to be formed from 'H' and 'L' Flights of No. 1 PRU under the command of Squadron Leader M.J.B. Young DFC.
'H' Flight of No. 1 PRU becomes 'A' Flight 540 Squadron
'L' Flight of No. 1 PRU becomes 'B' Flight 540 Squadron.

No. 1 PRU being disbanded.

The establishment of 540 Squadron to be Mosquito aircraft nine IE and two IRs to be increased at a later date to 18 IE and four IRs. Squadron HQ and 'A' Flight to be stationed at Leuchars and 'B' Flight to be stationed at Benson.

The Squadron is to be administered by No. 16 Group and to

come under RAF Station Benson. Flight Lieutenant M.D. Hood to be 'B' Flight commanding officer.

Introduction to 541 Squadron formation on 19 October 1942

Squadron to be formed from 'B' and 'F' Flights of No. 1 PRU under the command of Squadron Leader Stevenson with HQ in 'B' hangar.
The Squadron will be operating from Mount Farm.
'A' Flight commanding officer to be Flying Officer R. Cussons.
'B' Flight commanding officer to be Flying Officer Crakanthorp.

Introduction to 542 Squadron formation on 19 October 1942

'E' and 'A' Flights of No. 1 PRU at Mount Farm to become 'A' and 'B' Flights of 542 Squadron with offices and HQ in 'D' hangar at RAF Station Benson.

Introduction to 543 Squadron formation on 19 October 1942

Formed as one of the new Squadrons succeeding the disbanded No. 1 PRU. The Squadron to be under the command of Squadron Leader A.E. Hill DSO DFC. The Squadron will consist of two Flights and one HQ Section.
'A' Flight to be based at St Eval with Flight Lieutenant E.D.L. Lee as commanding officer.
'B' Flight to be based at Mount Farm with Flight Lieutenant F.A. Robinson DFC as commanding officer. Squadron HQ to be based at RAF Station Benson.

Introduction to 544 Squadron formation on 19 October 1942

The Squadron will consist of HQ and 'A' and 'B' Flights, 'B' Flight to be based at Gibraltar.
The Squadron aircraft strength to be as follows -

Flight Lieutenant
M.D. Hood. [See
page 56]

Squadron Leader
Antony E. Hill.
[See 21 October 1942]

Three Spitfires IV, two Wellingtons IV, Z1417 and Z1418
Five Ansons, one Tiger Moth and one Maryland.
The Spitfires to be held by 'B' Flight at Gibraltar.
The Ansons and Wellingtons to be held by 'A' Flight at Benson. The Ansons are to be used for communications and ferrying, and the Wellingtons are to be used for experimental night photography.

On 17 October 1943 all 544 Squadron Spitfires were transferred to 541 Squadron and the Squadron became fully equipped with Mosquitos.

19 October 1942   **543 Squadron 'A' Flight St Eval**

Sergeant Watson in Spitfire PR IV AA806 crashed on the aerodrome.

21 October 1942   **543 Squadron 'B' Flight at Mount Farm**

Squadron Leader A.E. Hill, commanding officer of 543 Squadron, took-off in Spitfire V AD121 at 1130 hours on sortie No. C526 to Le Creusot but failed to return. This sortie was allocated to 542 Squadron and their own aircraft. Squadron Leader Hill had been commanding officer of 543 Squadron for 2½ days.

Antony Eustace Hill DSO, DFC and Bar, RAFVR, s/n 72992, age 28, son of Colonel Eustace Hill DSO, TD, DL, MFH and Barbara Hill (née Gribble) of Ashwell, Hertfordshire. Buried in Dijon (Les Pejoces) Communal Cemetery, France. [Although squadron records show this sortie to have taken place on 21 October, the Commonwealth War Graves Commission lists Squadron Leader Hill's death as being on 12 November 1942.]

24 October 1942   **543 Squadron**

Flight Lieutenant G.E. Hughes DFC took over command of 543 Squadron wef 21 October 1942.

27 October 1942   **RAF Station Benson**

Sergeant Myles in Spitfire IV AB118, a pilot from another flight at Mount Farm, crashed at Benson due to misjudgement of height, resulting in Cat 'B' damage to the aircraft.

P.R. MOSQUITO CAMERA INSTALLATION

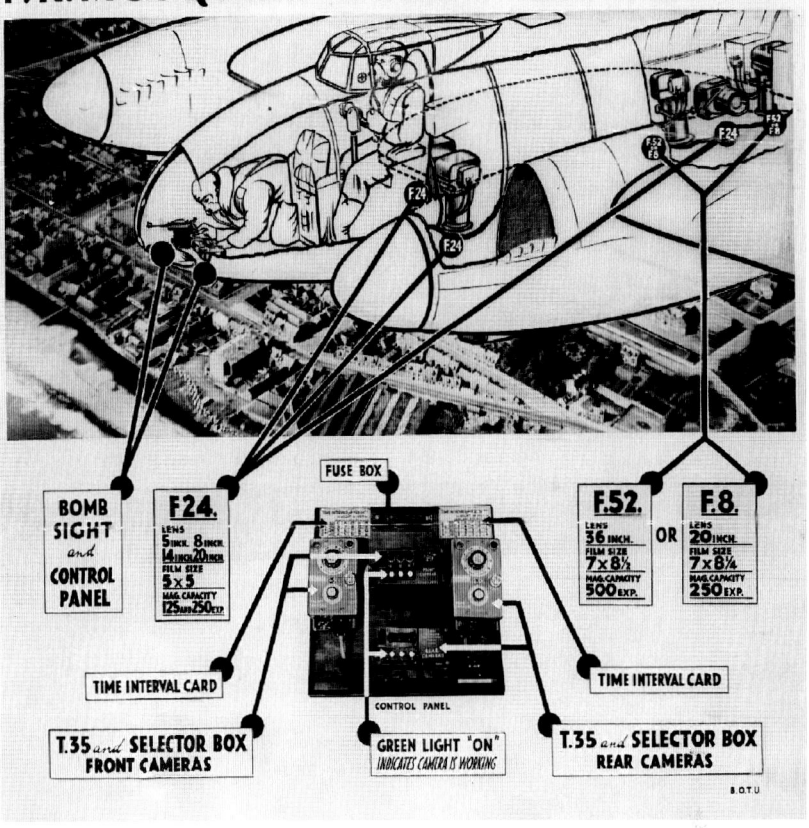

Film cassette.

27 October 1942   543 Squadron 'B' Flight at Mount Farm

Sergeant R.T. Luepke in Spitfire V AA806 took-off at 1430 hours on a sortie to Cherbourg and Le Havre but was shot down and failed to return.

Robert Theodor Luepke, s/n 605412, age 26, son of Otto and Lillian Luepke of Clarkedale, Arizona, USA. Died on 27 October 1942 and is commemorated on the Runnymede Memorial.

6 November 1942   541 Squadron

Pilot Officer L.J.E. Claert (Belgium) in Spitfire V AB309 took-off at 1145 hours on a sortie to Cherbourg and Le Havre but failed to return.

During October 1944 Pilot Officer Claert, who was formerly interned and now reclassified safe in UK, visited the Squadron. It appears he was shot down between Cherbourg and Le Havre by enemy fighters on 6 November 1942. He avoided capture and made his way to Belgium. Unfortunately owing to the fact that he had no identity discs he was refused aid by the [resistance] organization. Finally with a friend he reached Switzerland and was forbidden to leave until the Allies reached the Swiss frontier.

7 November 1942   540 Squadron

Pilot Officer Mortimer and Flight Sergeant Pike in Mosquito W4051 took-off at 1100 hours on a photo recce of Toulon and D/A at Genoa. There was cloud cover on track from the Channel to Nevers. Both targets were clear and photos were taken. After 45 minutes and before reaching the English coast the ASI went unserviceable and after that the main fuel ran out.

The pilot changed to outer tank and decided to land at the nearest aerodrome. The navigator was unable to contact base by W/T.

The pilot made a forced landing at Fairoaks aerodrome and skidded sideways into a stationary Blenheim causing it damage; his own aircraft damage was Cat A.C. The cameras and photographs were unharmed.

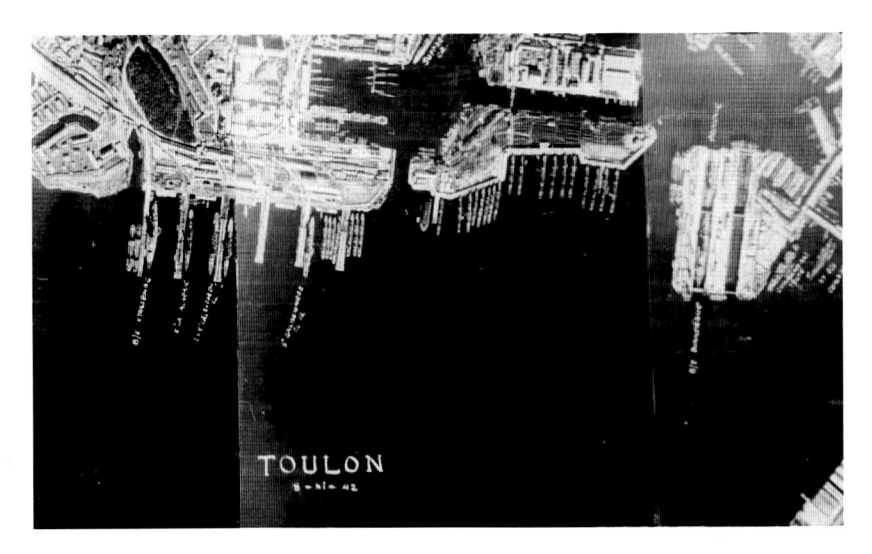

Photo of Toulon taken on 8 November 1942, the day after Pilot Officer Mortimer and Flight Sergeant Pike in Mosquito W4051, had to make a forced landing after their own trip to photograph Toulon.

The pilots of 'A' Flight, 541 Squadron with the Squadron Commander at Benson on Christmas Day 1942.

9 November 1942 — 544 Squadron 'B' Flight at Gibraltar

Flight Lieutenant C.A. Brennan in Spitfire BR666 took-off on a mission at 1100 hours to Casablanca and Marrakech but failed to return.

Charles Arthur Brennan, RCAF, s/n C/1448, age 26, son of Arthur and Florence Brennan of Summerside, Prince Edward Island, Canada. Died on 9 November 1942 and is commemorated on the Malta Memorial.

10 November 1942 — 544 Squadron 'B' Flight at Gibraltar

Pilot Officer W.R. Donaghue in Spitfire BR669 took-off at 0745 hours on a sortie to Phillippeville, Bone and Tunis but failed to return.

Although there was no record of Pilot Officer Donaghue having escaped either death or imprisonment, he is again shown as operating with 541 Squadron on 24 April 1944 and, on 14 September 1944, was posted to 8 OTU.

7 December 1942 — 542 Squadron

Flight Lieutenant F. Riley in Spitfire I R6964 took-off at 1334 hours on a sortie to a W/T objective near to Desvies but failed to return.

Frederick Riley, s/n 42024, age 30, son of George and May Riley of Manchester. Died on 7 December 1942 and is buried in Boulogne Eastern Cemetery, France.

8 December 1942 — 540 Squadron

Pilot Officer F.W. McKay and Flight Sergeant S.F. Hope in Mosquito DZ358 took-off for a photo recce of the Vienna area but failed to return.

Pilot Officer McKay, s/n 411424 of the RNZAF, in Mosquito DZ358 of 540 Squadron was captured and became a prisoner of war, number 85 at Stalag Luft III.

Flight Sergeant S.F. Hope, s/n 995562, of 540 Squadron was captured and became a prisoner of war, number 1247, in Stalag Luft VI.

1943

3 January 1943   140 Squadron

Sergeant A. Smith failed to return from a cross country flight to the Bristol Channel area in a Spitfire, having crashed at Northlew.

Arthur Smith, RAFVR, s/n 1213202, age 21, son of William and Hathalin Smith of Hinckley, Leicestershire. Died on 3 January 1943 and is buried in Hinckley Cemetery.

8 January 1943   541 Squadron

Pilot Officer A.G. Edwards in Spitfire V AB428 took-off at 1333 hours but later had trouble with his undercarriage and, on returning to base, he flew around for an hour under instructions from Flying Control. In the end however he was told to make a wheels up landing, which he did.

12 January 1943   541 Squadron Flight at Leuchars

Pilot Officer A.B. Anderson in Spitfire V R7041 took-off at 1145 hours on sortie N701 to Lister, Kristiansand and Kvasse Fjord but failed to return.

Pilot Officer A.B. Anderson, s/n 122332, in Spitfire R7041 of 541 Squadron was captured and became a prisoner of war, number 199, at Stalag Luft III.

13 January 1943   541 Squadron

Warrant Officer W.J. Payne in Spitfire IV R7044 took-off on an operations sortie to Stanlandet and Karno but failed to return; the take-off time was 1030 hours.

William John Payne, RAFVR, s/n 754956. Died on 13 January 1943 and is commemorated on the Runnymede Memorial.

25 January 1943   541 Squadron

Pilot Officer A.G. Edwards in Spitfire V BR660 took-off at 1115 hours on sortie No. C907. Due to engine trouble the pilot was forced to bale out at a position south-west of Guernsey at approx 1535 hours.

Allen Grayson Edwards, RAAF, s/n 416166, age 35, son of Allen and Maud Edwards of Hyde Park, South Australia. Died on 25 January 1943 and is commemorated on the Runnymede Memorial.

26 January 1943   542 Squadron

Sergeant J.D. Goldie in Spitfire PR IV AB430 took-off at 1305 hours on a sortie to the Ghent area but failed to return.

John Dunlop Goldie, RAFVR, s/n 1371755, age 22, son of Andrew and Janet Goldie of Cumnock, Ayrshire, husband of Agnes Goldie of Burnside, Rutherglen, Lanarkshire. Died on 26 January 1943 and is buried in Eeklo Communal Cemetery, Belgium.

4-5 February 1943   RAF Station Benson

The airfield was closed due to runway repairs.

7 February 1943   541 Squadron

Flying Officer J.C. Taffs in Spitfire XI EN385 took-off at 1000 hours on sortie No. C985 to Cologne and Düsseldorf but failed to return.

John Clifford Taffs, RAFVR, s/n 123031, age 21, son of Charles and Lily Taffs of Buckhurst Hill, Essex. Died on 7 February 1943 and is commemorated on the Runnymede Memorial.

8 February 1943   541 Squadron

Squadron Leader P.R.M. van der Heijden in Spitfire V BP881 took-off at 1030 hours on sortie No. C996 over Holland. It is believed that the aircraft was shot down off the Hook; wreckage was seen but no pilot.

Pieter Robert Marie van der Heijden, s/n 40190, son of Mr & Mrs P.H.J. van der Heijden. Died on 8 February 1943 and is commemorated on the Runnymede Memorial.

10 February 1943   541 Squadron
Sergeant F.J. Evans in Spitfire V AB125 took-off at 0940 hours on sortie D6 to Flushing, Rotterdam and the Hook but failed to return. He was reported as having been shot down by enemy aircraft at approximately 1050 hours, having previously been warned of the presence of enemy aircraft by Controller, Fighter Command. This message was acknowledged by the pilot who asked for their height immediately prior to being shot down.

No record of death for Sergeant F.J. Evans could be found but he may have been the Flight Sergeant F.J. Evans, s/n 1284654, who was captured and became a prisoner of war, number 312, at Stalag Luft VI.

13 February 1943   140 Squadron
Taking-off on a local sortie Flying Officer D. Croy crashed a Spitfire and was severely injured; the aircraft was a total loss.

Six months later, after 140 Squadron had moved to Hartford Bridge, Flying Officer Croy was killed in a formation flying accident.

Douglas Marchbank Croy, RNZAF, s/n 414259, age 22, son of James and Annie Croy of Oxford, Canterbury, New Zealand. Died on 5 August 1943 and is buried in Brookwood Military Cemetery.

13 February 1943   543 Squadron St Eval
Flying Officer G.B.D. Greenwood in Spitfire PR IV AA809 took-off at 1000 hours on a sortie to Lorient but failed to return.

George Benjamin Dudley Greenwood, RAFVR, s/n 118419, age 26, son of G. Benjamin and Kathleen Greenwood, husband of Betty Greenwood of Benson, Oxfordshire. Died on 13 February 1943 and is commemorated on the Runnymede Memorial.

Spitfire flown by Flying Officer D. Croy on 13 February 1943.

L to R: Sergeant Etherington, Charles Harris St John on the bicycle, Douglas Croy and Mac Davidson. [See 13 February 1943]

Mosquito I W4060 in which Flight Sergeant D. O'Neil and Sergeant A. Lockyer were lost. [See 20 February 1943]

Squadron Leader Van Der Heijden. [See 8 February 1943]

Sergeant J. Lavender. [See 4 March 1943.]

16 February 1943   541 Squadron

Sergeant J.P. Power in Spitfire I R7042 crashed at 1100 hours while on a practice cross country flight to Whitby; the pilot was killed.

James Patrick Power, RAFVR, s/n 1340974, age 20, son of Louis and Agnes Power of Peebles. Buried in Peebles Cemetery, Scotland.

17 February 1943   RAF Station Benson

Sergeant J.J. McCrohan, flying Spitfire BR417, crashed and was killed near Troon in Cornwall, while in transit from Portreath to Gibraltar.

John Joseph McCrohan, RAFVR, s/n 1316061, age 20, son of John and Kathleen McCrohan of Westcliff-on-Sea. Buried Leytonstone (St Patrick's) Roman Catholic Cemetery.

20 February 1943   540 Squadron Leuchars

Flight Sergeant D. O'Neil and Sergeant A.D. Lockyer in Mosquito PR I W4060 took-off at 1035 hours for Bergen and Stavanger but failed to return.

David O'Neil, RCAF, s/n R/92679, age 25, son of David and Jane O'Neil and husband of Jane O'Neil of Chester. Died on 20 February 1943 and is buried in Bergen (Mollendal) Church Cemetery, Norway.

Alfred David Lockyer, s/n 629806. Died on 20 February 1943 and is buried in Bergen (Mollendal) Church Cemetery, Norway.

20 February 1943   540 Squadron

Flying Officer W.L. Payne and Flight Sergeant A.J. Kent in Mosquito PR IV DZ466 took-off at 1010 hours for Vienna and the Linz area but failed to return. *See* 11 March 1943.

26 February 1943   542 Squadron

Flying Officer L. Xiezopolski in Spitfire F IX EN151 took-off at 0955 hours on a D/A sortie to Nuremburg but failed to return.

Flying Officer L. Xiezopolski, PAF, s/n P1418, flying Spitfire EN151 of 542 Squadron, was captured and became a prisoner of war, number 939, at Stalag Luft III.

26 February 1943   **543 Squadron St Eval**
Flying Officer R.W. Donaldson took-off in a Spitfire on an operational sortie but failed to return. No other details given.

Robert Wiseman Donaldson, s/n 31217, age 28, son of Alfred and Jeannie Donaldson, husband of Ethel Donaldson. Died on 26 February 1943 and is buried in Exeter Higher Cemetery, Devon.

28 February 1943   **543 Squadron St Eval**
Sergeant C.H. Evans in Spitfire PR IV AB128 took-off on an operational sortie to Bordeaux and the coastline to the north but failed to return.

Charles Hope Evans, RAFVR, s/n 1379807, age 20, son of Frederick and Marion Evans. Died on 28 February 1943 and is commemorated on the Runnymede Memorial.

3 March 1943   **541 Squadron**
Flying Officer G.R. Crakanthorp in Spitfire VII AR257 took-off at 1255 hours and made a successful sortie to Cherbourg. The aircraft was hit by enemy gunfire on the way home and the pilot was forced to make a crash landing at base at 1440 hours.

3 March 1943   **542 Squadron**
Flying Officer D.G. Scott crashed in a Spitfire XI while taking-off, due to a tyre bursting. There was Cat 'E' damage to the aircraft.

4 March 1943   **541 Squadron**
Sergeant R.M. Lawrence in Spitfire IV AB428, after returning from a sortie, made a forced landing near to Leighton Buzzard caused by a glycol leak in the engine.

4 March 1943   **541 Squadron**
Sergeant J. Lavender in Spitfire IV AA808 made a forced landing near to Aston Rowant. The operations report says that this was caused by a faulty manipulation of the petrol system. As a result the pilot was sent to the aircrew refresher school at Brighton and his log book was endorsed. Later, on 15 September 1943, Sergeant Lavender was promoted to Flight Sergeant wef

542 Squadron circa 1943.

Sergeant R.M. Lawrence
[See 4 March and 24 June 1943]

13 September 1942 and to Warrant Officer II wef 13 March 1943. The pilot carried out his first successful operation in Spitfire XI EN342 to the Amsterdam area on 5 April 1943.

6 March 1943   540 Squadron Gibraltar

Flying Officer D.F.I. Hardman and Sergeant B. Cruikshank in Mosquito IV DK315 took-off at 1035 hours on a transit flight to this country but went missing.

Donald Francis Ignatius Hardman, RNZAF, s/n 411888, age 26, son of Edward and Catherine Hardman of Dunedin, Otago, New Zealand. Died on 6 March 1943 and is commemorated on the Runnymede Memorial. [Although the squadron records show the date of death as 6 March 1943, the Commonwealth War Graves Commision shows it as 3 March 1943. It is likely that this was the date of departure from Gibraltar.]

Bernard Herbert Cruikshank, s/n 637524, age 35, son of George and Gertrude Cruikshank, husband of Sheila Cruikshank of Norbury, Surrey. Died on 6 March 1943 and is commemorated on the Runnymede Memorial. [Although the squadron records show the date of death as 6 March 1943, the Commonwealth War Graves Commision shows it as 3 March 1943. It is likely that this was the date of departure from Gibraltar.]

6 March 1943   542 Squadron

Flight Sergeant F.R. Duxbury in Spitfire BS501 took-off at 1400 hours on a sortie to the Essen area but failed to return.

Frederick Ronald Duxbury, RAFVR, s/n 1058490, age 21, son of John and Florence Duxbury, husband of Ivy Duxbury of South Ruislip, Middlesex. Died on 6 March 1943 and is buried in Bayeux War Cemetery, France.

11 March 1943   540 Squadron

Information has been received that Flying Officer Payne and Flight Sergeant Kent who were reported as missing on 20 February 1943 are now both prisoners of war.

Flying Officer W. Payne, s/n 101512, in Mosquito PR IV DZ466 of 540 Squadron was captured and became a prisoner of war, number 255, at Stalag Luft III.

Flight Sergeant A.J. Kent, s/n 1253865, in Mosquito PR IV DZ466 of 540 Squadron was captured and became a prisoner of war, number 27646, at Stalag 344 (formerly Stalag VIIIb).

12 March 1943   542 Squadron

Sergeant F. Lee in Spitfire IV BP929 took-off from base in coarse pitch and, failing to gain sufficient height, crashed into some trees. As a result his logbook was endorsed 'Gross Carelessness' and he was sent to the aircrew refresher school at Brighton.

13 March 1943   540 Squadron

Flying Officer P.J. Hugo and Pilot Officer M.L.H. Rose in Mosquito VIII DZ404 force landed at West Malling through engine failure, caused by enemy action. *See* 8 January 1944.

12-16 March 1943   140 Squadron

Between the above dates 140 Squadron moved from RAF Station Mount Farm to RAF Station Hartford Bridge.

15 March 1943   541 Squadron

Today the Squadron moved from Mount Farm to Benson.

18 March 1943   540 Squadron

Flight Sergeant M.M.U. Custance and Sergeant R.E. Smart in Mosquito PR VIII DZ364 took-off at 1330 hours for a recce sortie of Brux but failed to return.

Flight Sergeant M.M.U. Custance, s/n 1387822, of 540 Squadron, was captured and became a prisoner of war, number 895, at Stalag Luft VI.

Sergeant R.E. Smart, s/n 1092622, of 540 Squadron, was captured and became a prisoner of war, number 919, at Stalag Luft VI.

18/19 March 1943   RAF Station Benson

Halifax DG283 of 161 Squadron crash landed at Henley-on-Thames as a result of engine failure. Two of a crew of seven were killed.

28 March 1943   540 Squadron

Flight Lieutenant N.D. Sinclair and Flying Officer W. Nelson in Mosquito PR I W4054 took-off at 1052 hours for a sortie to the Trondheim area but failed to return. *See* 23 April 1943.

Members of 542 Squadron pose for the camera. L to R top: Flying Officer B.J. McMaster, Pilot Officer 'Gale' Whitaker, Flight Lieutenant Whitehead. Bottom: Flight Sergeant Hunter, Pilot Officer A. Grubb and Pilot Officer G.B. Singlehurst.

28 March 1943 — 542 Squadron

Flying Officer D.E. Wilson in Spitfire F IX EN348, after returning from a sortie, was forced to make a crash landing at base due to aircraft damage by enemy action. Pilot took-off at 1145 hours and landed at 1830.

30 March 1943 — RAF Station Benson

An accident involving three people and two aircraft occurred today. Squadron Leader R.V. Whitehead from RAE at Farnborough, having taken-off to return to his station, crashed on to 542 Squadron dispersal with the result that Flight Lieutenant B.J. McMaster DFC, officer commanding 'B' Flight 542 Squadron, and Leading Aircraftman T. Bedford, together with Squadron Leader Whitehead were all killed. The aircraft was burnt out and an aircraft of 542 Squadron, standing at dispersal, was slightly burnt.

Roy Valentine Whitehead DFC, s/n 41086, age 30, son of Ambrose and Elizabeth Whitehead, husband of Joan Whitehead of Oxford. Buried in Brookwood Military Cemetery.

Brian John McMaster DFC, s/n 8444696, age 27, son of John and Devina McMaster, husband of Mary McMaster of St Ippolyts. Buried in Ippollitts (St Ippolyt) New Churchyard.

Thomas Bedford, RAFVR, s/n 1384160, age 28, son of Thomas and Ellen Bedford, husband of Lena Bedford of East Ham. Buried in Leytonstone (St Patrick's) Roman Catholic Cemetery.

3 April 1943 — 540 Squadron Leuchars

Pilot Officer J.D. Mair and Pilot Officer D.E. George in Mosquito PR IV DZ487 took-off at 1355 hours for Oslo, Horten and Kristiansand but failed to return.

John Drysdale Mair DFC, RAFVR, s/n 138437, son of John and Rachel Mair of Clydebank, Dumbartonshire. Died on 3 April 1943 and is commemorated on the Runnymede Memorial.

Daniel Ernest George, RAFVR, s/n 121564. Died on 3 April 1943 and is commemorated on the Runnymede Memorial.

3 April 1943 — 541 Squadron

Pilot Officer G.C.D. Hunter in Spitfire XI EN149 took-off at 1530 hours on a sortie and, upon returning, had to make a forced landing at Manston due to the engine cutting at high altitudes. The aircraft landed at 1800 hours.

9 April 1943 — 540 Squadron

A Mosquito IV piloted by Sergeant A. Campbell swung during a cross wind take-off. The aircraft was considerably damaged but the crew were uninjured.

10 April 1943 — RAF Station Benson

A defence scheme 'Exercise Faith' was laid on as from 1300 hours today when the stand-to was ordered; action stations followed at 1700 hours; a practice gas attack and air raid warning at 2130 hours and the all clear and raiders past was given at about 2215 hours.

The night passed without incident but during the morning of the 11th the battle was resumed. At 1030 hours the station was attacked by 600 Home Guards representing parachute troops. From 1100 hours to 1300 hours all personnel on the station manned their 'Attack Alarm Posts'. Members of aircrew formed into Mobile Command Units under the command of Wing Commander S.L. Ring DFC and went into action in the final phase.

13 April 1943 — 541 Squadron

Flying Officer J.R. Brew in Spitfire IV BR415, while on a test flight and during circuit, was unable to lower his flaps, consequently he decided on a no flaps landing, inadvertently landing wheels up as well.

The operations report says that whilst circumstances were extenuating it was, nevertheless, a bad show by a pilot of his experience.

16 April 1943 — 540 Squadron

Sergeant J.G. Parkinson swung off the runway when landing Mosquito I W4051 damaging props and undercarriage. The crew found it difficult to get out of the aircraft. *See* 7 July 1943.

16 April 1943 — 541 Squadron

Sergeant W. Johnson in Spitfire IV AA807 on landing back from a sortie tipped the aircraft over on its nose; only slight damage resulted.

19 April 1943 — RAF Station Benson

Compulsory PT for all ranks, twice a week, commences today.

22 April 1943 — RAF Station Benson

Notification has been received of the decision by HQ Coastal Command to form No. 309 Ferry Training and Aircraft Dispatch Unit at this station forthwith.

23 April 1943 — RAF Station Benson

A Whitley bomber of No. 10 OTU, when attempting to land in poor visibility, overshot and crashed into a gun pit.

23 April 1943 — 540 Squadron

Information has been received from International Red Cross that Flight Lieutenant N.D. Sinclair DFC of 'A' Flight at Leuchars, reported missing on 28 March 1943, is now a POW. Flying Officer W. Nelson DFC (Observer) is reported killed.

Flight Lieutenant N.D. Sinclair, s/n 42897, in Mosquito W4054 of 540 Squadron was captured and became a prisoner of war, number 990, at Stalag Luft III.

Wilfred Nelson DFC, RAFVR, s/n 112719, age 31, son of Herbert and May Nelson of Heaton Chapel, Stockport, Cheshire. Died on 28 March 1943 and is buried in Trondheim (Stavne) Cemetery, Norway.

24 April 1943 — 540 Squadron

Squadron Leader G.E. Hughes in Mosquito VIII DZ342 swung on take-off from Church Fenton where he had force landed. There was extensive damage to the undercarriage and propellers.

3 May 1943 — 540 Squadron

Wing Commander The Lord M.A. Douglas-Hamilton OBE is re-posted to the Squadron.

3 May 1943   **540 Squadron**

Warrant Officer T.J. Moss and Pilot Officer G.N. Sutton in Mosquito PR IV DZ532 took-off at 1030 hours on a sortie to the Breslau area but failed to return.

Thomas John Moss, s/n 521717, age 26, son of Edwin and Edith Moss, husband of Megan Moss of Cardigan, Wales. Died on 3 May 1943 and is commemorated on the Runnymede Memorial.

George Nevil Sutton, RAFVR, s/n 125815, age 24, son of George and Elizabeth Sutton of Fulwood, Lancashire. Died on 3 May 1943 and is commemorated on the Runnymede Memorial.

5 May 1943   **RAF Station Benson**

Sergeant G.A. Rich in a Spitfire XI, while ferrying from Portreath to Gibraltar force landed on a beach in Portugal near to Oporto due to icing and engine trouble. The station has been notified that the pilot is well and that he was able to destroy all secret equipment.

9 May 1943   **RAF Station Benson**

'Exercise Skylark' was carried out today. Briefly the scheme was to drop a number of aircrew within a seven mile radius of the station to test their ability to get back to camp without being challenged. Local Police and Home Guard cooperated in large numbers and only two of the escapists succeeded in reaching the Guard Room undetected. The exercise was considered to have been most useful and the following conclusions were drawn:

> 1. There was a marked tendency to become overconfident after early success.

> 2. Tiredness caused lack of concentration.

> 3. The small compasses were extraordinarily accurate.

14 May 1943   **540 Squadron**

Flight Sergeant R.B. Shepherd and Flight Sergeant H.W. Evans in Mosquito PR IV DZ523 took-off at 1100 hours for D/A of Pilsen but failed to return.

Reginald Bernard Shepherd, RAFVR, s/n 656280, age 23, son of Henry and Alma Shepherd of Herne Bay, Kent. Died on 14 May 1943 and is buried in Longuyon Churchyard, France.

Since no details could be found for either the death or the imprisonment of Flight Sergeant Evans it is likely that he escaped and returned to the United Kingdom.

15 May 1943   540 Squadron

Flight Lieutenant J.H. Loder and Flight Sergeant T.J. Hughes in Mosquito PR IV DZ494 took-off at 2225 hours on a sortie over Northern France but failed to return.

John Harrington Loder DFC, RAFVR, s/n 86357, age 25, son of John and Gladys Loder of Lenham, Kent. Died on 15 May 1943 and is buried in Boulogne Eastern Cemetery, France.

Trevor Jones Hughes, RCAF, s/n J/17635, age 30, son of John and Mary Hughes of Winnipeg, Manitoba, Canada. Died on 15 May 1943 and is commemorated on the Runnymede Memorial.

18 May 1943   RAF Station Benson

During the past three days PR aircraft from this station have obtained magnificent photographs of the Eder and Möhne dams which were breached by Bomber Command on 16/17 May 1943.

Flying Officer F.G. 'Jerry' Fray in Spitfire XI EN343 of 542 Squadron took-off at 0725 hours on 17 May and returned 3 hours and 35 minutes later having taken one of the most famous photographs of the war – that of the breached Möhne dam. For his part in the operation Flying Officer Fray was awarded the DFC.

19 May 1943   RAF Station Benson

Wing Commander V.H.P. Lynham DSO, Wing Commander training at No. 16 Group, visited the station today for further discussions on the formation of No. 309 FT and ADU.

The cast of RAF Benson Dramatic Society's production of *The Ghost Train*. Back row: far left Jean Ratcliffe, far right Jean Daly. Middle row: Stan Carssons (or Jay Jay Brown), Bob Taylor, Eric Thompson, Joan Stevens, Duncan Wilson, Freddie Efford, Jay Jay Brown (or Stan Carssons). Front row: Jerry Fray, Ruth Fray, Eric Searle, Hilda Smith, Micky Lewis, Tommy Turnbull. [See 18 May 1943 and Appendix IX]

Squadron Leader D. Salwey who lost his life in a mid air collision over Nettlebed near Benson. [See 6 June 1943]

20 May 1943   540 Squadron

Sergeant A. Campbell and Sergeant J. Arkle of 540 Squadron were killed this afternoon when their Mosquito crashed near Newbury. Failure of the port engine is believed to be the cause.

Archibald Campbell, RAFVR, s/n 1371720, age 29, son of Archibald and Isabella Campbell of Perth, Scotland. Buried in Perth (Wellshill) Cemetery.

James 'Jimmy' Arkle, RAFVR, s/n 1109187, age 21, son of James and Edith Arkle of Ripon. Buried in Ripon Cemetery.

28 May 1943   542 Squadron

Sergeant T. Goulden in Spitfire F IX EN411 took-off at 1715 hours on an operational sortie to Hamburg and Lübeck but failed to return.

Thomas Goulden, RAFVR, s/n 1044413, age 24, son of Thomas and Isabella Goulden of North Shields, Northumberland. Died on 28 May 1943 and is commemorated on the Runnymede Memorial.

6 June 1943   542 Squadron

Squadron Leader D. Salwey DFC and Flight Lieutenant B. Clegg DFC were killed in a mid air collision during practice formation flying. The incident was over Nettlebed. Squadron Leader Salwey baled out but had insufficient height to make a successful drop.

David Salwey DFC, s/n 33399, age 24, son of the Revd Geoffrey and Hildegard Salwey of Botley Rectory. Died on 6 June 1943 and is buried in Botley (All Saints) Churchyard.

Bernard Clegg DFC, s/n 33536, son of James and Doris Clegg of Thornes, Wakefield. Died on 6 June 1943 and is commemorated at Leeds (Lawns Wood) Crematorium.

8 June 1943   RAF Station Benson

Air Commodore Boothman AFC takes command of the station.

12 June 1943   RAF Station Benson

At 1340 hours Aircraftman 1st Class J. Phypers was found shot dead in the adjutant's office of 541 Squadron. Service and civil police are investigating.

John Phypers, RAFVR, s/n 1611663, age 39, son of Alfred and Annie Phypers of Acton, Middlesex. Died on 12 June 1943 and is buried in Benson (St Helen) Churchyard Extension. An inquest into the death of Aircraftman Phypers was held on 16 June 1943 and the verdict was that he had committed suicide by shooting himself with a Service revolver while the balance of his mind was disturbed.

13 June 1943   541 Squadron
Sergeant W. Johnson in Spitfire XI BS490 took-off on sortie No. D671 to the Dortmund Ems Canal at 0600 hours but failed to return.

Sergeant W. Johnson, s/n 1295901, of 541 Squadron was captured and became a prisoner of war, number 35, at Stalag Luft VI.

13 June 1943   540 Squadron
Sergeant A.G. Wright and Sergeant G.G. Lane in Mosquito PR IV DZ438 took-off at 1130 hours for photo recce of the Corunna area but failed to return.

Arthur George Wright, RAFVR, s/n 1336470, age 21, son of Arthur and Kate Wright of Shoeburyness, Essex. Died on 13 June 1943 and is commemorated on the Runnymede Memorial.

Geoffrey George Lane, RAFVR, s/n 1322909, age 22, son of Charles and Dorothy Lane of Thornton Heath, Surrey. Died on 13 June 1943 and is commemorated on the Runnymede Memorial.

16 June 1943   541 Squadron
Sergeant A.B. Depree in Spitfire XI MB782 on a transit flight from Portreath to Gibraltar force landed in Portugal.

18 June 1943   541 Squadron
Sergeant V.I. Gorrill in Spitfire XI MB790 took-off at 0910 hours on a sortie to Oberhausen and Essen. On its return the aircraft was intercepted by two FW190s which fired bursts from long range causing slight damage to the aircraft. The pilot made a forced landing at Ludham [Norfolk] at 1240 hours.

23 June 1943   544 Squadron
Squadron Leader W.R. Acott DFC force landed in Tiger Moth R4958; the pilot was uninjured.

Sergeant V.I. Gorrill, front right. [See 18 June 1943]

Flying Officer, later Squadron Leader W.R. Acott. [See 23 June 1943]

24 June 1943   541 Squadron

Sergeant R.M. Lawrence in Spitfire XI MB792 took-off at 0530 hours on sortie No. D731 to Kiel but failed to return. A distress signal was sent from somewhere over the North Sea, just off the Hook of Holland, but no more was heard from the pilot.

Ralph Maurice Lawrence, RCAF, s/n R/103250, age 25, son of James and Hilda Lawrence of Brantford, Ontario, Canada. Died on 24 June 1943 and is buried in Flushing (Vlissingen) Cemetery, Holland.

24 June 1943   540 Squadron

Sergeant P.D. Thomas was the pilot of Mosquito DZ383 when, 20 miles north-west of Lake Geneva, the starboard engine cut and smoke and flames issued from the exhausts. The pilot feathered the propeller and turned onto a reciprocal course losing height. On the homeward journey he dived to cool the port engine which became very hot and rough. He also unfeathered the starboard propeller but the engine immediately overheated so it was feathered again. The aircraft maintained height at 15,000 feet until 20 miles from the north French coast where the pilot dived to gain speed. He landed safely at base having flown 480 miles in 2 hours 40 minutes on the port engine only.

26 June 1943   RAF Station Benson

Today 106 PR Wing was formed at the station and will become effective as of 3 July 1943.

30 June 1943   541 Squadron

Sergeant H.K. Shawjer in a Spitfire IX burst a tyre on take off necessitating a wheels up landing.

3 July 1943   106 PR Wing

As previously reported, 106 PR Wing was formed and becomes effective today. The Wing will be responsible for RAF Station Benson; Nos. 540, 541, 542, 543 and 544 Squadrons; 309 FT and ADU, Benson, and 8 OTU Dyce. Administration of the units in the Wing will be undertaken by HQ 16 Group.

Appointments to the Wing are as follows:
>	Air Commodore J.N. Boothman AFC as AOC
>	Wing Commander S.L. Ring DFC as Senior Operations Staff Officer
>	Wing Commander R.C. van der Ben as Senior Officer Administration duties
>	Squadron Leader W.R. Acott DFC as Operations Senior Officer
>	Squadron Leader P.H. Watts DSO DFC as Staff Training Officer

3 July 1943   **543 Squadron**

Flying Officer H.J. Rothwell in a Spitfire II took-off at 0953 hours on a sortie to the Bordeaux area. He abandoned the aircraft approximately 30 miles south of the Lizard. Air Sea Rescue units failed to locate the pilot.

Herbert Jack Rothwell, RAFVR, s/n 128452, age 28, son of Herbert and Frances Rothwell, husband of Ada Rothwell of Cheetham, Manchester. Died on 3 July 1943 and is commemorated on the Runnymede Memorial.

4 July 1943   **RAF Station Benson**

A Halifax II JB856 of 77 Squadron, returning from a raid on Cologne, landed at the station early this morning with a smashed starboard elevator and damaged tailplane. The mid upper gunner, Sergeant A. Cuthbertson, was killed and the rear gunner, Sergeant C.M. Goudy (RCAAF) was severely injured and later died.

Alfred Cuthbertson, RAFVR, s/n 1384688, age 22, son of Henry and Ellen Cuthbertson of Canning Town. Died on 4 July 1943 and is buried in Leytonstone (St Patrick's) Roman Catholic Cemetery.

C. McKenzie Goudy DFM, s/n R/139157. Died on 17 July 1943 and is buried in Oxford (Botley) Cemetery.

7 July 1943   **540 Squadron**

Sergeant J. G. Parkinson crashed a Mosquito while on a test flight. The aircraft swung after a precautionary landing and the undercarriage collapsed.

1943

8 July 1943   **RAF Station Benson**

A message of thanks for the volume of photographs dealing with the recent attack on the German Dams, has been received today from HM the King's Private Secretary.

11 July 1943   **540 Squadron, Leuchars**

Flying Officer D.F. Quirt and Flying Officer J.H. Benton in Mosquito PR IV DZ517 took-off at 0615 hours for Bergen. On the return the aircraft crashed into hills near to Montrose. Flying Officer Benton was killed and Flying Officer Quirt was seriously injured.

John Hudson Benton, RCAF, s/n J/9761, age 29, son of Frank and Frances Benton of Victoria, British Columbia, Canada. Died on 11 July 1943 and is buried in Leuchars Cemetery, Scotland.

11 July 1943   **540 Squadron, Leuchars**

Flying Officer E.F. Kirwan and Flying Officer W.M. Fergusson in Mosquito PR IV DZ419 took-off at 0617 hours for a photo recce of Kristiansand. On their return the aircraft came down off the coast by Arbroath in heavy mist. Both members of the crew are missing.

Edmund Francis Kirwan, RAFVR, s/n 1188436, age 28, son of the Hon. Sir John Waters Kirwan MLC JP and Lady Kirwan (née Quinlan) of Perth, Western Australia. Died on 11 July 1943 and is buried in Leuchars Cemetery, Scotland.

William Meiklejohn Fergusson, RAFVR, s/n 132340. Died on 11 July 1943 and is buried in Leuchars Cemetery, Scotland.

15 July 1943   **541 Squadron**

Sergeant V.B. White came down in the sea two miles off Cromer when returning from a sortie. He was rescued by the Air Sea Rescue Service.

16 July 1943   **540 Squadron**

Flying Officer G.E. Mann and Flying Officer D.W. Licquorish in Mosquito PR IV DZ431 took-off at 1100 hours on an operational sortie but failed to return.

Geoffrey Edward Mann, RAFVR, s/n 125981, age 20, son of Thomas and Mabel Mann of Tunbridge Wells, Kent. Died on 16 July 1943 and is buried in Milan War Cemetery, Italy.

Donald Webster Licquorish, RAFVR, s/n 129591, age 23, son of Albert and Gladys Licquorish of West Molesey, Surrey. Died on 16 July 1943 and is buried in Milan War Cemetery, Italy.

28 July 1943　　　　　　　　　544 Squadron

Flight Sergeant R. Watson and Flight Sergeant A.L. Reynolds in Mosquito IV DZ600 took-off at 2320 hours on a sortie. On their return, when within six miles of the camp, they were shot down by a friendly night fighter and both crew members were killed.

Russell Watson, s/n 530636, age 27, son of Trevor and Harriet Watson, husband of Nellie Watson. Died on 29 July 1943 and is buried in Bedford Cemetery.

Arthur Lumley Reynolds, RAFVR, s/n 1112033, age 29, son of Harold and Mary Reynolds of Manningham, Bradford, husband of Mollie Reynolds of Manningham. Died on 29 July 1943 and is buried in Calverley (St Wilfrid) Churchyard.

5 August 1943　　　　　　　　　543 Squadron

Flying Officer K.R. Holland, in Spitfire IV BR412, force landed at Abingdon due to engine failure.

10 August 1943　　　　　　　540 Squadron, Leuchars

Pilot Officer F.V. Legon, in Mosquito XIII DZ404 force landed at Leuchars due to port engine failure.

18 August 1943　　　　　　　　540 Squadron

Flying Officer S.I. Baird force landed at Benson in Mosquito PR IX LR412 due to engine failure through loss of oil.

23 August 1943　　　　　　　RAF Station Benson

Air Commodore Boothman and Wing Commander Ring tested Westland Welkin aircraft at Boscombe Down for PR suitability on 10 August and 19 August but today the new Westland Welkin was rejected by Air Commodore Boothman on account of its lack of speed and its poor operational view.

3 September 1943 — RAF Station Benson

A Wellington aircraft from RAF Station Oakley crashed near to Watlington. The crew of six were all killed.

24 September 1943 — 540 Squadron

Pilot Officer J.H. Williams and Flight Sergeant E.P.H. Peek in Mosquito PR IX LR405, took-off on an operational sortie but failed to return.

James Henry Williams, RAFVR, s/n 148816, age 23, son of James and Irene Williams, husband of Constance Williams of Stourbridge, Worcestershire. Died on 24 September 1943 and is buried in Zwollerkerspel (Voorst) General Cemetery, Holland.

Ernest Percy Henry Peek, RAFVR, s/n 1375401, age 23, son of Percy and Bertha Peek of Walthamstow, Essex. Died on 24 September 1943 and is buried in Zwollerkerspel (Voorst) General Cemetery, Holland.

17 October 1943 — 544 Squadron

As from today all Squadron Spitfires were transferred to 541 Squadron and 544 Squadron became fully equipped with Mosquitos.

18 October 1943 — 543 Squadron

Squadron Disbanded

The disposal of the Squadron as follows.

'A' Flight at St Eval to be taken over by 541 Squadron, the aircraft to be distributed between Nos. 541 and 542 Squadrons. The pilots will also be distributed between the same squadrons.

'B' Flight at Benson will cease to exist, ground crews to be distributed between 542 and 544 Squadrons, and some from 'B' Flight to be attached to 309 FT and ADU. It was 'B' Flight who originally developed this unit, training crews for overseas duties.

20 October 1943 — RAF Station Benson

A fire tender and a crash party went to Ipsden where a Stirling aircraft EF497 from 90 Squadron crashed and caught fire.

26 October 1943   540 Squadron, Leuchars

Acting Squadron Leader R.A. Lenton MC DFC and Pilot Officer R.S. Haney in Mosquito PR IX LR420 took-off at 1100 hours on a sortie to the Trondheim area but failed to return.

Reginald Arthur Lenton MC, DFC, s/n 42315, age 28, son of Edward and Lucy Lenton. Died on 26 October 1943 and is commemorated on the Runnymede Memorial.

Robert Shirley Haney, RAFVR, s/n 146288, son of John and E. Margaret Haney of Earlsdon, Coventry. Died on 26 October 1943 and is commemorated on the Runnymede Memorial.

31 October 1943   RAF Station Benson

The briefing and interrogation section of intelligence moved from the old mansion house at Ewelme to SHQ. This section is now known as operational intelligence. The photographic intelligence section remains at the old mansion house at Ewelme.

2 November 1943   170 Squadron

The above squadron, formed at Weston Zoyland in 1942, began tactical reconnaissance missions equipped with Mustangs at the beginning of 1943 and today carried out its first operation from Benson following a temporary posting here. The operation was the inland 'Popular' mission.

3 November 1943   RAF Station Benson

Air Commodore Boothman and Squadron Leader Ring delivered a Fortress aircraft that had been damaged and repaired at Benson airfield, to Thorney Island.

3 November 1943   544 Squadron

Flight Sergeant J. Walker and Flight Sergeant J.W.S. Henderson in Mosquito PR IX LR436 on returning from a sortie, crashed at Leith Hill, Surrey, and both crew were killed.

John Walker, RAFVR, s/n 1347996, age 21, son of John and Isobel Walker of Edinburgh. Died on 3 November 1943 and is commemorated at Edinburgh (Warriston) Crematorium.

James William Sutherland Henderson, RAFVR, s/n 1024228, age 29, son of James and Margaret Henderson (née Sutherland) of Brucklay. Died on 3 November 1943 and is buried in Old Deer Cemetery.

4 November 1943   541 Squadron

Flying Officer R.O. MacLean (RAAF) in Spitfire XI MB908 took-off at 1005 hours on sortie No. S990 to the Bordeaux area but failed to return.

Roderick Orr MacLean RAAF, s/n 409611, age 26, son of Roderick and Jeanetta MacLean of Caulfield, Victoria, Australia. Died on 4 November 1943 and is commemorated on the Runnymede Memorial.

11 November 1943   544 Squadron, Gibraltar

Wing Commander D.C.B. Walker and Flying Officer A.M. Crow in Mosquito PR IX LR478 took-off at 1114 hours on a sortie to Modane but failed to return.

Donald Cecil Broadbent Walker, formerly Captain, Royal Northumberland Fusiliers, s/n 25126, age 28, son of Lawrence and Jessie Walker of Woodlands, Malton, Yorkshire. Died on 11 November 1943 and is buried in Pena (Navarre) Cemetery, Spain.

Flying Officer A.M. Crow survived, escaped capture and returned to the United Kingdom. See 29 December 1944 for further details.

23 November 1943   170 Squadron

Flying Officer F.C. Yearwood took-off at 1000 hours in Mustang FD504 on an operations sortie. When near to his objective he hit a tree but managed to get home and land at Ford. The aircraft was badly damaged.

25 November 1943   541 Squadron

Warrant Officer K.G. Campbell in Spitfire XI EN154 and Flight Sergeant D. Gravenstede in Spitfire XI EN417, while on a sortie in the Boulogne area, were intercepted and chased by a number of Thunderbolts.

November 1943   541 Squadron

541 Squadron took over the southern area which was covered by 'A' Flight from Benson. Operations from St Eval and Gibraltar

were carried out by 'B' Flight based at St Eval with a detachment at Gibraltar. In the area covered by 'A' Flight, operation 'Crossbow' arose, necessitating recces of numerous pinpoints and areas in a coastal strip about 100 miles deep from the Pas de Calais to the Cherbourg peninsula. Operations by 'A' Flight from Benson were over Belgium, Holland, Denmark and northern Germany as far east as Berlin and Leipzig.

1 December 1943   542 Squadron
Flying Officer P.J. Spencer in Spitfire XI MB789 flew into a hill near to Henley in bad weather and was killed.

Peter John Spencer, RAFVR, s/n 158319, age 20, son of William and Daisy Spencer of Hayes, Middlesex. Buried in Oxford (Botley) Cemetery.

1 December 1943   544 Squadron
Flight Lieutenant A.S. Pilcher (RCAF) and Flying Officer D.F. Robins took-off in Mosquito PR IX LR419. When the aircraft was three miles south-west of West Malling an intense 'blue' note was heard, suggesting that the aircraft dived into the ground from a considerable height. The crew were both killed.

Alan Swaine Pilcher, RCAF, s/n C/1078, age 24, son of Commander H.B. Pilcher RN and Hilda Pilcher of Fort Steele, British Columbia, Canada. Buried in Brookwood Military Cemetery, Surrey. [The Commonwealth War Graves Commission shows the date of death as 2 December 1943.]

Donald Frederick Robins, RAFVR, s/n 151265, age 33, son of Frederick and Lucilla Robins, husband of Dorothy Robins of Prestbury, Cheltenham, Gloucestershire. Buried in Brookwood Military Cemetery, Surrey. [The Commonwealth War Graves Commission shows the date of death as 2 December 1943.]

10 December 1943   63 Squadron
The first mention of the squadron on the operations sheet since April 1940, as detachments began to move in to RAF Station Benson.

Above: The Old Mansion, Ewelme.
Below: Photographic Intelligence buildings in the grounds.

Photographic Intelligence staff. Back row, L to R: ACW Payne, ACW White, ?, ?; Middle row: Sgt Upstone, ?, F/O Oldfield, F/O Thomas, Sgt Dagworthy, Cpl Fuller: Front row: F/O Flux, Flt Lt Robertson, Flt Lt Tozer, Sqn Ldr Weaver, Flt Lt Craig, Flt Lt Hornby, F/O Hennesy and the dog, Touser.

Squadron Leader Smith Lewis of the Photographic Section.

Photographic Intelligence room at the Old Mansion in Ewelme.

Tea break time for some of the ground crews.

16 December 1943 — 541 Squadron, Gibraltar

Flight Lieutenant R.P. Johnson, officer commanding Squadron detachment, took-off shortly before noon for the UK in Spitfire BS491. The aircraft crashed at 1415 hours at Wraxall in Somerset. The pilot was found one mile from the aircraft; his parachute had not been used and it was suspected that he had been hit by some part of the aircraft after baling out.

Roy Percival Johnson, RAFVR, s/n 67059, age 26, son of Richard and Ellen Johnson, husband of Elfreda Johnson of Addington village. Died on 16 December 1943 and is buried in Addington (St Mary) Churchyard, Surrey.

18 December 1943 — 541 Squadron

Flight Lieutenant S.L.E.G. Gheude (Belgium) failed to return from a sortie to Hamburg in Spitfire PR XI EN669.

Flight Lieutenant S.L.E.G. Gheude, s/n 108611, of 541 Squadron was captured and became a prisoner of war, number 1783, at Stalag IXc.

21 December 1943 — 63 Squadron

Flying Officer Ray in Mustang IA took-off at 1245 hours. Later the aircraft was hit by flak and the pilot had to bale out.

22 December 1943 — 170 Squadron

170 Squadron left this station today and their operations are taken over by 63 Squadron, being used to obtain low level photographs of special targets.

31 December 1943 — RAF Station Benson

Five Flying Fortresses landed at the station today due to a lack of fuel, and bad visibility after a raid on Bordeaux and Cognac. One aircraft landed with its bombs still on board.

Spitfire XI EN154. [See 25 November 1943]

'B' Flight of 541 Squadron at St Eval, Cornwall.

1944

January 1944   **RAF Station Benson**

Squadron Leader A.H.W. Ball DSO DFC assumes the duty of Staff Training Officer and Squadron Leader Watts takes up a wing commander post at 8 OTU Dyce.

January 1944   **106 Wing HQ**

An improvement in visibility on Mosquito aircraft must be accomplished as an operational requirement, as enemy aircraft can approach from the rear without the pilot or observer being aware of their presence. It is considered feasible to introduce a perspex upper blister to the escape hatch, to obtain the required sighting and the modification is being arranged through appropriate Air Ministry channels.

4 January 1944   **544 Squadron**

Flight Sergeant M.L. Bartley and Flight Sergeant D.B. Perman in Mosquito IX MM232 took-off at 1315 hours on a sortie to St Dizier. They were attacked by enemy fighters over France and failed to return. No definite information was received as to what happened to them beyond a Coastal Y report which stated that a parachute had been sighted at 1555 hours in the Poix area. This was approximately on Bartley's track and at approximately the correct time. The necessary signal action was taken.

Maxwell Logan Bartley, RNZAF, s/n 415679, age 23, son of Alva and Alice Bartley of Auckland, New Zealand. Died on 4 January 1944 and is buried in Poix-de-Picardie Churchyard.

There are no further details of Flight Sergeant D.B. Perman although there is a record of a prisoner of war, B.R. Perman, who was held at Stalag 4B, Muhlberg, Elbe, which may refer to him.

Above: The Operations room at RAF Station Benson.
Below: The Debriefing room.

8 January 1944   540 Squadron
Flying Officer P.J. Hugo and Flying Officer M.L.H. Rose in Mosquito PR IX LR407 returned from a sortie and, as a result of an accident near to Benson, crashed and both crew members were killed.

Peter John Hugo, RAFVR, s/n 122131, age 21, son of Dr Harold F.L. Hugo and F. Bessie Hugo of Crediton, Devon. Buried in Benson (St Helen) Churchyard Extension.

Merton Lambert Horfield Rose, RAFVR, s/n 124222, age 25, son of Lambert and Ida Rose of Shrewsbury, Shropshire. Buried in Benson (St Helen) Churchyard Extension.

21 January 1944   63 Squadron
The detachment left for North Weald en route for Scotland.

21 January 1944   541 Squadron
Flight Sergeant J. Aitken in Spitfire XI EN503 took-off on an operations sortie at 1055 hours to the Pas de Calais but failed to return.

James McGinn Aitken, RAFVR, s/n 1552265, son of James and Agnes Aitken of Dalry, Ayrshire, Scotland. Died on 21 January 1944 and is commemorated on the Runnymede Memorial.

29 January 1944   544 Squadron
Squadron Leader B.G. Aston and Flight Lieutenant P.S.A. Fielding in Mosquito PR IX LR430 took-off at 1845 hours on a sortie to the Le Mans marshalling yards but failed to return.

Squadron Leader B.G. Aston, s/n 42328, in Mosquito LR430 of 544 Squadron was captured and became a prisoner of war, number 3461 at Stalag Luft III.

Peter Samuel Ashton Fielding, s/n 46819, age 31, son of Douglas and Lily Fielding, husband of Joyce Fielding of Grimsby, Lincolnshire. Died on 29 January 1944 and is buried in Le Mans West Cemetery, France.

February 1944   106 Wing HQ
Further deliveries of the rear view blisters for Mosquito IX aircraft are urgently requested to enable 100 per cent fitment for

squadrons of 106 Wing. An incident has been reported where the incorporation of the blister definitely saved an aircraft from possible destruction by an enemy aircraft.

The necessity for securing pressure cabins for PR aircraft was again represented and, as their provision would entail a different type of crank case of Rolls-Royce engines, the AOC met representatives of the firm. The two essentials of all PR work are great speed and great ceiling. Had the Mosquito had the ability of the Spitfire to fly at great heights, pilots would have been able to persist with sorties which they have had to abandon owing to persistent condensation trails; non persistent trail regions would have been entered and missions continued. Another reason for great height is that high-flying fighters now escort daylight bomber missions and PR aircraft must be able to get well above these. The Mosquito cannot operate in this manner, therefore sorties are cancelled or, alternatively, crews are pushed to very considerable risks.

It is not considered at this HQ that Merlin 76 or 77 engines will overcome this disability but what is to be aimed at is to increase the ceiling by 4,000-5,000 feet and the speed by 25 mph. The Mosquito will thus be brought within hailing distance of the new Spitfire. Fitting of 16 SM Merlin engines, extended wing tips, new airscrews and reduction of AUW can be envisaged. Until this type of aircraft arrives HQ considers the Mosquito performance to be unsatisfactory.

9 February 1944   540 Squadron

Flying Officer M. Ostoja-Slonski and Acting Flight Lieutenant P. Riches in Mosquito PR IX LR412, crashed into Aran Fawddwy mountain near Dolgelly in Merionethshire while on a test flight. Both crew members were killed.

Paul Riches DFC, RAFVR, s/n 119442, age 23, son of James and Catherine Riches, husband of Peggy Riches of Kingston-on-Thames. Buried in Chessington (St Mary) Churchyard.

Flying Officer Marek Ostoja-Slonski, PAF, s/n P1953, age 29, of Tarnów, Poland is buried in Chessington (St Mary) Churchyard in the same grave as Flight Lieutenant Riches. His two brothers, Jerzy age 31 and Bogdan age 22, also flew with the Royal Air Force, both being killed in

1941. Although Flying Officer Ostoja-Slonski's name is shown this way on his gravestone, Polish sources indicate that the surname should be shown as Slonski-Ostoja.

19 February 1944   540 Squadron

Flying Officer S.C. Urquhart and Flying Officer E.C. Braun in Mosquito III LR522 crashed at South Easton and were both killed.

Stanley Clarke Urquhart, RAFVR, s/n 141843, age 31, son of William and Emily Clarke Urquhart, husband of Anne Urquhart of Edinburgh. Died on 19 February 1944 and is buried in Bath (Haycombe) Cemetery.

Edward Charles Braun, RAFVR, s/n 124840, age 30, son of Adolphe and Martha Braun of Romford, Essex. Died on 19 February 1944 and is buried in Bath (Haycombe) Cemetery.

23 February 1944   RAF Station Benson

An enemy aircraft, which crashed at Andridge Farm near Stokenchurch last night, was found. Two unidentified German airmen were buried at Benson Extension churchyard with full military honours. The author was one of the pall-bearers. The airmen were only identified after the end of the war.

Grefreiter [Aircraftman 1st Class] Karl-Heinz Borowski, born in Wilhelmshaven on 25 November 1924. Died on 22 February 1944 while on a raid against London and was buried in Benson (St Helen) Churchyard Extension.

Leutnant [Pilot Officer] Felix Müller, born in Böhlitz-Ehrenberg on 3 October 1909. Died on 22 February 1944 while on a raid against London and was buried in Benson (St Helen) Churchyard Extension.

In February 1963 the bodies of the two airmen were exhumed and reburied at the German Military Cemetery at Cannock Chase, Staffordshire.

25 February 1944   542 Squadron

Flying Officer G.W. Puttick in Spitfire XI PA855 ran out of fuel over France on his return journey. The pilot managed to glide

Mosquito PR IX of 540 Squadron.

The graves of two German airmen who died when their aircraft crashed at Andridge Farm.
[See 23 February 1944]

back and landed in an orchard near RAF Station Manston. The aircraft was badly damaged. The pilot sustained slight head injuries.

25 February 1944   542 Squadron
Flight Sergeant H.F. Buckingham in Spitfire XI BS502 took-off at 1040 hours on a sortie over the Pas de Calais but failed to return.

Henry Francis Buckingham, RAFVR, s/n 1322657, age 22, son of Charles and Florence Buckingham of Dagenham, Essex. Died on 25 February 1944 and is commemorated on the Runnymede Memorial.

February 1944   541 Squadron
On 9 February one pilot found his aircraft covered with little white spots after climbing through alto stratus cloud at 22,000 feet over the North Sea. The wind was a strong northerly and had been for some days. On analysis the deposit was found to be sodium nitrate. Again on 12 February at 30,000 feet in a clear sky and northerly wind, another pilot reported a slight deposit in this area.

1 March 1944   RAF Station Benson
A Wellington X aircraft, LN614, belonging to RAF Harwell crashed near Cholsey at approximately 0300 hours but was not reported until 0900 hours. Five of the crew were killed and the one surviving crew member was taken to the Royal Berks Hospital at Reading.

7 March 1944   RAF Station Benson
Horsa Glider I HG755 crashed at Henley, map reference 186042 Sht 105. All action taken by parent unit No. I Glider Pilot Regiment at Stoney Cross.

13 March 1944   540 Squadron
Wing Commander Lord M.A. Douglas-Hamilton is posted from the station and Squadron Leader J.R.H. Merifield DSO DFC is promoted to wing commander and made Commanding Officer of 540 squadron.

19 March 1944　　　　　　　　**RAF Station Benson**
The new station cinema and theatre was opened today.

21 March 1944　　　　　　　　**RAF Station Benson**
A Dakota FL597 of 512 Squadron crashed at Model Farm, North End near Watlington, map reference 172127 Sht 105, at about 1130 hours. Four of the crew were killed; the remaining member, Flying Officer J.C. Beck died the next day. No details given for other crew members.

John Creighton Beck DFM, s/n 52694, age 23, son of John and Robina Beck of Dumfries. Died on 22 March 1944 and is buried in Dumfries (St Andrew's) Roman Catholic Cemetery.

31 March 1944　　　　　　　　**RAF Station Benson**
A Halifax III LW579 of 51 Squadron crashed at Cowleaze Wood near Stokenchurch. The crew of five were all killed. No other details given.

7 April 1944　　　　　　　　**544 Squadron, Leuchars**
Flight Sergeant D.N. Howarth and Flight Sergeant S.S. Kelley in Mosquito IX MM247 took-off at 0720 hours on a mission over northern Europe but failed to return.

David Norman Howarth, RAFVR, s/n 1086884, age 21, son of David and Elisabeth Howarth of Preston, Lancashire. Died on 7 April 1944 and is commemorated on the Runnymede Memorial.

Stanley Kelley, RAFVR, s/n 1581082. Died on 7 April 1944 and is buried in Varobacka Church Cemetery, Sweden.

8 April 1944　　　　　　　　**544 Squadron**
Flying Officer G.C.D. Hunter and Flying Officer J. Fielden in Mosquito IX MM239 returning from San Severo to Benson, crashed on take-off. The crew were unhurt but the aircraft suffered Cat 'B' damage.

10 April 1944　　　　　　　　**540 Squadron**
Flying Officer F.V. Legon and Pilot Officer J.W. Swann in Mosquito IX LR424 took-off at 1555 hours for Friedrichshafen but failed to return.

Frederick Vernon Legon, RAFVR, s/n 128578, age 24, son of Albert and Martha Legon of Balham, London. Died on 10 April 1944 and is buried in Verdun-sur-Meuse (Faubourg Pave) French National Cemetery.

Pilot Officer J.W. Swann, s/n 161040, was captured and became a prisoner of war, number 5108, at Stalag Luft III.

10 April 1944   542 Squadron

Pilot Officer E.R. Cumming in Spitfire XI EN330 took-off at 1745 hours on a sortie to the Abbeville area but failed to return.

Ernest Robert Cumming, RCAF, s/n J/18599, age 21, son of Thomas and Frances Cumming, husband of Lillian Cumming of Marton, Blackpool, Lancashire. Died on 10 April 1944 and is commemorated on the Runnymede Memorial.

13 April 1944   540 Squadron

Flying Officer C.C. Drew AFC and Flight Sergeant J.I. Shaer in Mosquito PR IX LR416 were both killed in a flying accident at Kingston Bagpuize at 1108 hours.

Charles Cyril Drew, RCAF, s/n J/23033, age 27, son of Dr J.M. Drew BA MB ChB and Ruth Rae Drew. Died on 13 April 1944 and is buried in Brookwood Military Cemetery, Surrey.

Joseph Israel Shaer, RAFVR, s/n 1294047, age 24, son of Samuel and Clara Shaer. Died on 13 April 1944 and is buried in Oxford (Wolvercote) Cemetery.

14 April 1944   542 Squadron

Flight Sergeant H.A. King in Spitfire XI EN424 took-off at 1320 hours on a sortie over Dieppe and Le Havre but failed to return.

Herbert Allan King, RAFVR, s/n 605474, age 25, son of George and Beatrice King of St Michael, Barbados, British West Indies. Died on 14 April 1944 and is commemorated on the Runnymede Memorial.

18 April 1944   541 Squadron, Gibraltar

Flight Sergeant H.M. Rittman in Spitfire II PR777 force landed at Larache in French Morocco due to a fuel shortage; the pilot is safe and uninjured.

21 April 1944 — RAF Station Benson

Authority received for formation of No. 106 Group wef 14 April 1944.

21 April 1944 — RAF Station Benson

Group Captain C.E. Beamish St John DFC reported to Benson from HQ Coastal Command as Station Commander.

24 April 1944 — 541 Squadron

Flight Lieutenant W.R. Donaghue in Spitfire XI EN668 set off for the Ruhr but his engine cut repeatedly at 37,000 feet so he turned for home. On his return journey the engine cut at 36,000 feet and restarted at 24,000 feet at a fairly wide throttle opening. While the pilot was on instruments in rough cumulonimbus cloud the aircraft was flying on one side, the hood was torn off and the door flew open; all the instruments spun and, for a while, the pilot lost control. He centralized his controls and broke cloud at 11,000 feet in a very fast spiral dive. He pulled the aircraft out of the dive as carefully as possible but, even so, by using two hands. He was down to 1,000 feet before regaining straight and level flight. When the aircraft landed the wings were found to be badly buckled on their top surfaces and the fuselage was strained.

29 April 1944 — RAF Station Benson

Leading Aircraftman A. Allonby FME of No. 2 Group Communications Flight, a lodger unit at Benson, was killed as a result of an accident when he was struck by a 542 Squadron Spitfire MB902.

Arthur Allonby, RAFVR, s/n 1017481, age 28, son of Lancelot and Annie Allonby of Askern. Died on 29 April 1944 and is buried in Askern Cemetery.

April 1944 — RAF Station Benson

It is noteworthy that during the month of April the first issues of the following new Spitfires for preparation and reallocation to No. 106 Group Squadrons were made. Spitfire PR X similar to PR XI but is equipped with pressure cabin. Spitfire PR XIX equipped with the new Rolls-Royce Griffon Mk. 65 engine.

Flying Officer Gordon W. Puttick of 542 Squadron who failed to return from a sortie to Hanover and Paderborn. 542 Squadron records noted: 'The loss of a very valuable pilot was felt by all.' It was later discovered that he had become a prisoner of war. [See 25 February and 13 May 1944]

The farm at Preston Crowmarsh, near Benson, where Lancaster III ND989 of No. 50 Squadron crashed into the farmhouse on 20 May 1944.

10 May 1944   RAF Station Benson

A fire occurred in Mosquito LR406 of 544 Squadron in 'B' hangar, due to the accidental firing of a Very pistol, with only slight damage to the aircraft.

10 May 1944   540 Squadron

Flying Officer J.H. Irwin and Flying Officer L. Moody in Mosquito IX LR421 took-off at 0730 hours for the Munich area but failed to return.

Jack Hector Irwin, RAAF, s/n 409709, age 21. Died on 10 May 1944 and is buried in Klagenfurt War Cemetery, Austria.

Leopold Moody, RAFVR, s/n 151395, age 32, son of Leopold and Margaret Moody, husband of Winifred Moody of Fulwood, Preston, Lancashire. Died on 10 May 1944 and is buried in Klagenfurt War Cemetery, Austria.

13 May 1944   542 Squadron

Flying Officer G.W. Puttick, in Spitfire XI EN685, took-off at 1400 hours on a sortie over the Hanover and Paderborn areas but failed to return.

Gordon W. Puttick, s/n 124541, of 542 Squadron, survived the crash of his aircraft to become a prisoner of war. His camp and POW number are unknown.

15 May 1944   540 Squadron

Flying Officer P.N. Farlow and Pilot Officer E.G.G. Boyd in Mosquito IX LR408 took-off at 1000 hours on an operational sortie but failed to return.

Both of these officers survived to become prisoners of war. Their POW numbers and camp details are unknown.

20 May 1944   RAF Station Benson

A Lancaster III ND989 of No. 50 Squadron crashed at 0420 hours. The aircraft was coming in to land but undershot the runway and crashed in an orchard, hitting a house at Preston Crowmarsh. The aircraft, which had been diverted due to bad weather at its base, was returning from a raid. Pilot Officer J.R.

Irving, Sergeant F.D. Jewell and Sergeant F.I. Drever were all killed and the remaining four members of the crew suffered shock and slight injuries.

John Robert Irving, RAFVR, s/n 174403, age 22, son of Melita Irving and stepson of Ernest Fullard of New Bilton Grange, Hull. Died on 20 May 1944 and is buried in Hull Eastern Cemetery.

Francis Douglas Jewell, RAFVR, s/n 1506251, age 22, son of Mrs & Mrs John Jewell of Rothwell. Died on 20 May 1944 and is buried in Rothwell Cemetery, Yorkshire.

Frederick Irving Drever, RAFVR, s/n 1557888840, age 20, son of George and Louisa Drever of Leith, Edinburgh. Died on 20 May 1944 and is buried in Edinburgh (Seafield) Cemetery.

24 May 1944   544 Squadron

Pilot Officer W. Kennedy and Flight Sergeant L. Chambers in Mosquito II LR434 took-off at 0505 hours on an operations sortie to the Berlin area but failed to return. During the day unofficial information was received that the aircraft had made a forced landing at Ystad in southern Sweden at 0900 hours, the crew being uninjured. *See* 30 August 1944 and report below.

The following may well typify the experiences of other crews and the hazards of flying on photographic sorties in unarmed PR aircraft.

Mosquito LR 434 – 544 Squadron
24 May 1944
near Ystad in Sweden

On the 24th of May 1944 I, with my observer F/Sgt L. Chambers, was detailed by PRU intelligence to obtain photographic cover of airfields in the Berlin and Brandenburg areas. I took-off from Benson at 0500 hours in Mosquito LR 434 from 544 Squadron. I crossed the English coast near Coltishall at 28,000 feet at 0530 hours and pre-pointed on track along the Frisian Islands, crossing in at St Peter, Denmark at 0620 hours. At St Peter I set course for the first airfield target about 50 miles north of Brandenburg. The cloud was 6/10ths but [the] target was photographed. I then set course for two other airfields near Brandenburg and successfully covered these. Here I was subjected to normal but very accurately predicted flak which continued for about 15 minutes while tracking past Berlin. Evasive action was taken at intervals when bursts came too near for comfort, but flak was almost continually behind although accurate for height.

My next airfield was about 20 miles north-east of Berlin and about 1 minute after covering this, while tracking towards Berlin, I was subjected to a terrific barrage, each salvo of 300-400 bursts. It was impossible to avoid the second of these salvos by taking evasive action, as by this time I was flying through the bursts, one of which hit the belly of the aircraft, pieces of shrapnel bursting my glycol tanks and severely damaging my port engine which had to be feathered as soon as I cleared the concentration. My port engine, which had been on fire, cleared after about 3 minutes, so the aircraft was not abandoned but I set course north for Sweden, flying on my starboard engine which was starting to heat up, owing to loss of coolant. Airspeed of 190-200 miles was maintained but height was being lost at approximately 300 feet per minute.

About 4 minutes after feathering my port engine I was intercepted by a Ju 88 which was coming, head on, towards me at 20,000 feet. I ordered my navigator to prepare to leave the aircraft as we carried no guns and we were flying on one engine; we should have been a sitting target to the enemy aircraft. As the Ju 88 approached to about 100 yards I decided to try a bluff, so flew straight towards him in a friendly manner and I even went so far as to waggle my wings. This seemed to fox him, or probably he mistook me for a Me 210 as no head on attack was made and we passed each other wing tip to wing tip. I ordered my navigator to keep an eye on the Ju 88, which he did and warned me when it turned into attack after overshooting me by about 5 miles. The chase now started but having obtained this lead in the right direction I opened up my starboard engine flat out and dived the Mosquito towards some wisp of cloud of about 6/10ths at 13,000 feet. The Ju 88 was now gaining on me but

I entered the cloud before he could fire. I continued to fly through this thin cloud but eventually ran into the clear finding, by some excellent luck, I had lost the Ju 88.

My starboard engine was now in very bad shape but I continued towards Sweden, losing height steadily. I crossed the German coast at Swinemünde at approximately 0840 hours at 8,000 feet and made the sea crossing to Sweden without further incident, except a prayer for my starboard engine which was now terribly overheated, spluttering badly and threatening to catch fire.

I crossed the Swedish coast at 4,000 feet about 5 miles west of Ystad losing height steadily. I was now looking for a field in which to crash land, as the aircraft was too low to bale out. The aircraft landed nicely but broke up, the nose and side as well as the windshield and instrument panel were all smashed up and the tail broke off near the rear. The IFF detonator buttons were pushed and my navigator jettisoned the top hatch and got clear of the aircraft. I had a little more trouble as the stick and other equipment were jamming me in my seat.

I released myself in about a minute, pulled out the 2 incendiary bombs and climbed out on to the wing tip above the petrol tank. The first bomb fizzled but appeared to be damp and eventually went out, being U/S.

By this time Swedish Home Guards had arrived and tried to pull me off the mainplane. They did not succeed until after I had the second bomb going, and set it on the petrol tank. I was pulled well clear of the aircraft by the Swedish Home Guard only to find that a civilian ran back to the aircraft, tossed clear the burning bomb and extinguished the fire with a bucket of water. F/Sgt Chambers and myself were then taken by the Swedish military to Ystad where we spent one night at the Continental hotel before journeying the next evening to Falun, escorted by a Swedish captain.

Signed 172775 P/O W. Kennedy Pilot.

Rubber models of the D-Day landing beaches made with the aid of photographs taken by PR pilots.

Danesfield House – RAF Medmenham in Buckinghamshire, which was home to the Central Interpretation Unit.

28 May 1944   **542 Squadron**

Flying Officer N.R.M. Clark in Spitfire XI MB788 took-off at 1815 hours on a sortie over the Siegfried Line and the Geldern area but failed to return.

Neville Roy Maslen Clark, RAAF, s/n 21614, age 26, son of William and Dorothy Clark, husband of Phyllis Clark of Leichhardt, NSW, Australia. Died on 28 May 1944 and is buried in Jonkerbos War Cemetery, Holland. [The Commonwealth War Graves Commission shows the date of death as 29 May 1944.]

1 June 1944   **541 Squadron**

Flying Officer J.R. Campbell in Spitfire PR XI MB902 crashed on a transit flight from Benson to St Eval. The aircraft was found wrecked on high ground west of Devizes. The pilot was killed.

James Russell Campbell, RAFVR, s/n 155796. Died on 1 June 1944 and is buried in Llandudno (Great Orme's Head) Cemetery.

8 June 1944   **RAF Station Benson**

Halifax LW128 of 429 Squadron crashed ½ mile north-east of Benson airfield. Squadron Leader W.B. Anderson (RCAF) was killed. Three other crew members successfully baled out and were admitted to Benson Station Sick Quarters and treated for slight shock. The remaining three members of the crew are reported to have baled out over the continent.

William Brodie Anderson, RCAF, s/n J/8924, age 30, son of Dr Robert Anderson MD and Margaret Anderson of West Kildonan, Manitoba, Canada. Died on 8 June 1944 and is buried in Brookwood Military Cemetery, Surrey.

9 June 1944   **544 Squadron**

Flying Officer J.A. Downie and Flight Sergeant V.G. Ross in Mosquito PR XVI MM352 were on a low level D/A behind the battle lines in southern France but failed to return.

James Alexander Downie, RAFVR, s/n 162947, age 24, son of William and Mary Downie of Acton, Middlesex, husband of Nita Downie (née Priestman). Died on 9 June 1944 and is buried in Romagne Communal Cemetery, France.

Victor Gwyn Ross, RAFVR, s/n 177269, age 21, son of Annie Ross and stepson of Cyril J. Hemming of Splott, Cardiff. Died on 9 June 1944 and is buried in Romagne Communal Cemetery, France.

14 June 1944 RAF Station Benson
Acting Squadron Leader E.D.L. Lee DFC posted from No. 106 PR Group as the new Commanding Officer of 309 FT and ADU.

15 June 1944 541 Squadron
Squadron Leader J.H. Saffery in Spitfire XIX RM633 took-off at 0605 hours for a sortie to the Ruhr. The pilot baled out over the English Channel and was picked up by MTB 605 at 2240 hours.

10 July 1944 544 Squadron, Leuchars
Flying Officer E.S. Simonson (RCAF) and Flying Officer W. Reid in Mosquito XVI MM365 crashed on return from a mission at 1900 hours at Mulben between Rothes and Keith. Both members of the crew were killed.

Ernest Stanfield Simonson, RCAF, s/n J/23023, age 27, son of Mr & Mrs R. Simonson, husband of Muriel B. Simonson of Regina, Saskatchewan, Canada. Died on 10 July 1944 and is buried in Banff Cemetery, Scotland.

William Reid, RAFVR, s/n 135289, age 30, son of George and Isabel Reid (née Elrick), husband of Gladys Reid (née Le Moine) of Aberdeen. Died on 10 July 1944 and is buried in Banff Cemetery, Scotland.

12 July 1944 544 Squadron, Leuchars
Flight Lieutenant F.L. Dodd, pilot, and Flight Sergeant E. Hill, observer, took-off at 1225 hours from Leuchars airfield in Mosquito XVI NS505 of 544 Squadron on the first stage of a long endurance flight, sortie No. 106 G/L.13, to photograph the German battleship *Tirpitz*, sheltering in Kaa Fjord on the Norwegian coast, as a follow up to a heavy bombing raid carried out by a force of Lancaster bombers.

The aircraft was fuelled up to its capacity of 873 gallons, of which 866 gallons were useable. Drop tanks were fitted and the fuel was distributed as follows:

Two Outer Wing Tanks @ 49 gallons	98 gallons
Two Inner Wing Tanks @ 144 gallons	288 gallons
Two Drop Tanks @ 100 gallons	200 gallons
Fuselage Tank	136 gallons
Bomb Bay Tank	151 gallons
Total	873 gallons

After an uneventful flight, Flight Lieutenant Dodd landed at Sumburgh at 1335 hours and was airborne again at 1425 hours, taking the great circle track to Alten Fjord, flying at a height of approximately 27,000 feet at plus 2½ boost and 2300-2400 revs. This pattern was maintained as far as within 69 degrees of this point. When over Alten Fjord the aircraft descended to 10,000 feet and, as the cloud base was now at 9,000 feet, Flight Lieutenant Dodd brought the aircraft down below this level in preparing to make a photographic run. The top hatch then blew off causing considerable consternation to the crew.

The run continued with vertical and oblique cameras running and on a second run made over Kaa Fjord with all vertical cameras on and further obliques taken, the crew sighted the *Tirpitz*.

The battleship was inside double booms with a second naval unit adjacent on the north side of the battleship, also inside the booms. A third naval unit was sighted alongside booms some distance away, north-east of the Kaa Fjord, whilst east of the *Tirpitz* approximately four destroyers were sighted. During a second run over the target one of these destroyers opened fire on the aircraft with no effect.

Flight Lieutenant Dodd climbed the aircraft back to an altitude not exceeding 20,000 feet, to avoid excessive cold due to the absence of the top hatch. During the return journey a tanker was sighted in the south end of Skjomen Fjord. This vessel was photographed and obliques of the body taken.

No further incidences occurred and the aircraft landed at Wick at 2205 hours and, after a brief stop for refuelling, took-off again for Leuchars where it landed at 2325 hours.

When Flight Lieutenant Dodd and his observer landed at Wick they had been airborne for a period of 7 hours 40 minutes, with only 10 gallons of fuel left in the aircraft.

The aircraft was a normal operational PR Mosquito XVI fitted with 72 and 73 Rolls-Royce Merlin engines.

Summary of sortie times as follows:

Take-off Leuchars	1225 hours
Landed Sumburgh	1335 hours
Take-off Sumburgh	1425 hours
Crossed enemy coast Landegode	1700 hours
Over target *Tirpitz*	1800 hours
Landed Wick	2205 hours
Take-off Wick	2245 hours
Landed Leuchars	2325 hours

Later Flight Lieutenant F.L. Dodd was awarded the DSO and Flight Sergeant E. Hill was awarded the DFM.

18 July 1944   544 Squadron

Flight Lieutenant W. Hampson and Pilot Officer G.N.E. Newby in Mosquito IX LR431 took-off on an operations sortie to Leipzig, Osnabrück and Brunswick but failed to return.

Flight Lieutenant W. Hampson, s/n **86696**, was captured and became a prisoner of war, number **4793**, at Stalag Luft I.

Pilot Officer G. Newby, s/n **176746**, was captured and became a prisoner of war, number **4800**, at Stalag Luft I.

18 July 1944   RAF Station Benson

Halifax III LK794 of 578 Squadron crashed near Bisham. Six members of the crew are missing, believed killed. The station provided a crash guard.

25 July 1944   544 Squadron

Flight Lieutenant A.E. Wall and Flying Officer A.S. Lobban in Mosquito XVI MM273 took-off at 1655 hours on an operations sortie. They were attacked for 20 minutes by an Me262 and eventually broke away in cloud at 16,000 feet over the Tyrol. A course was then set on escape maps to Italy and they made an emergency landing at Fermo on the shores of the Adriatic. *See* 25 March 1945.

Flight Lieutenant John Weaver, OC Intelligence Section.

ASO Delia Britain, Intelligence Section, using a stereoscope to obtain a 3D picture from two overlapping photographs.

ASO Weightman, Intelligence Section.

ASOs Thompson and Chalmers, Plotting Section.

ASO Laws, Plotting Section.

2 August 1944   RAF Station Benson

A Lightning from Mount Farm crashed near Benson airfield killing the pilot. No other details are known.

2 August 1944   542 Squadron

Flight Sergeant R.H. Kershaw in Spitfire XI EN682, after being attacked by enemy fighters over Holland and Belgium, crashed at 2035 hours at Dunsfold. No other details are known.

2 August 1944   544 Squadron

Squadron Leader Lord David Douglas-Hamilton and Flying Officer P.E. Gatehouse in Mosquito PR IX MM240 crashed at South Moreton near Didcot at 1540 hours.

David Douglas-Hamilton, RAFVR, s/n 73704, age 32, son of Alfred Douglas Douglas-Hamilton, 13th Duke of Hamilton, 10th Duke of Brandon, and the Duchess of Hamilton (née Poore); husband of Lady Douglas-Hamilton (née Stack). Died on 2 August 1944 and is buried in Berwick St John (St John the Baptist) Churchyard.

Philip Edwin Gatehouse DFM, RAFVR, s/n 131888, age 31, son of Ernest and Alice Gatehouse of Swaythling, Southampton. Died on 2 August 1944 and is buried in Oxford (Botley) Cemetery.

6 August 1944   544 Squadron

Flight Lieutenant J.S. Towsey and Flying Officer R.J. Kingham in Mosquito XVI NS504 failed to return from a sortie to Paris and Lyons.

John Stanley Jack Towsey, RAFVR, s/n 86330, age 29, son of Charles and Jessie Towsey, husband of Catherine Towsey of Cefn Cribbwr, Glamorgan. Died on 6 August 1944 and is buried in Lyon (La Doua) French National Cemetery.

Richard John Kingham, RAFVR, s/n 143099. Died on 6 August 1944 and is buried in Lyon (La Doua) French National Cemetery.

8 August 1944   540 Squadron

Flight Lieutenant D.L. Matthewman DFC and Flight Sergeant W.D. Stopford in Mosquito PR IX LR433 took-off at 1120 hours for Munich but failed to return.

Viewing the film   The film drum

Processing the photographs taken by the PR crews

Printing   Drying and glazing

Desmond Laurence Matthewman DFC and Bar, RAFVR, s/n 101013, age 23, son of Thomas and Florence Matthewman of Cheam, Surrey. Died on 8 August 1944 and is buried in Durnbach War Cemetery, Germany.

William Douglas Stopford, RAFVR, s/n 969477, age 24, son of Sidney and Eunice Stopford, husband of Bessie Stopford of Handforth, Cheshire. Died on 8 August 1944 and is buried in Durnbach War Cemetery, Germany.

9 August 1944   540 Squadron
Flight Lieutenant J.L.H. Richards and Pilot Officer R.J. Barents in Mosquito PR IX LR435 took-off at 0915 hours for Gdynia and Danzig but failed to return. *See* 30 August 1944 and 1 April 1945.

11 August 1944   542 Squadron
Flight Lieutenant R.W. Atkinson DFC was posted to No. 16 Squadron to fill a squadron leader post but was killed the next day. He was struck by a propeller while walking on the perimeter track.

Ronald William Atkinson DFC, RAFVR, s/n 43537, age 25, son of William and Ethel Atkinson of New Southgate. Died on 12 August 1944 and is commemorated at Golders Green Crematorium, London.

11 August 1944   544 Squadron
Flight Lieutenant D. Adcock and Flying Officer G.D. Askew in Mosquito IX MM245 took-off at 1618 hours for a low level oblique of a 'No Ball' supply site at Fôret de Nieppe but failed to return.

Douglas Adcock, RAFVR, s/n 43246, age 30, son of Cecil and Violet Adcock of Redhill, Surrey. Died on 11 August 1944 and is buried at Middelkerke Communal Cemetery, Belgium.

George Douglas Askew, RAFVR, s/n 151269, age 21, son of George and Dinah Askew of Longsight, Manchester. Died on 11 August 1944 and is commemorated on the Runnymede Memorial.

15 August 1944   RAF Station Benson
Three escaped Russian prisoners of war arrived at the station

from the USAAF at Mount Farm. They were transferred the next day to the Disposal Centre at Wandsworth.

19 August 1944   544 Squadron

Flying Officer H.R. Vickers (RAAF) and Flight Sergeant M.A. Mossley in Mosquito XVI MM354 were attacked and the aircraft damaged in elevators, ailerons, cockpit and both engines by two Me190s in the Paris area. The pilot opened up and dived, leaving the enemy aircraft behind. After a few minutes one engine failed and would not feather and the pilot could only maintain height at 200 feet with the good engine flat out. The good engine failed suddenly after 40 minutes when the aircraft was on the top of a wood. The pilot mushed the aircraft into the top of the wood whence it ended up in a turnip field minus engines, mainplanes, nose and tail. Flying Officer Vickers broke an ankle. The crew were picked up by an American advanced patrol in no man's land after a few minutes and were eventually flown back to this country. Flying Officer Vickers rang Benson during the morning of 21 August 1944.

21 August 1944   540 Squadron

Warrant Officer K.L. Boyd (NZ) and Flight Sergeant H.R. Read in Mosquito XVI MM360 took-off at 1330 hours to Stettin but failed to return.

Kenneth Leslie Boyd, RNZAF, s/n 411381, age 24, son of Robert and Minnie Boyd of Grey Lynn, Auckland, New Zealand. Died on 21 August 1944 and is commemorated on the Runnymede Memorial.

Howard Richard Read, RAFVR, s/n 1395940, age 34, son of Richard and Florence Read of Walberton, Sussex. Died on 21 August 1944 and is commemorated on the Runnymede Memorial.

23 August 1944   540 Squadron

Flight Lieutenant T.R. Jenkins and Flight Sergeant D.C. Dawson in Mosquito XVI MM355 took-off at 1630 hours for a wireless station near to Den Helder but failed to return.

It is believed that Flight Lieutenant Jenkins may have become a prisoner of war but no other details are known.

Dennis Charles Dawson, RAFVR, s/n 1580354, age 21, son of Samuel and Elsie Dawson of Stone Staffordshire; husband of Elaine Dawson of Walton, Stone. Died on 23 August 1944 and is commemorated on the Runnymede Memorial.

30 August 1944   RAF Benson

Information has been received that Flight Sergeant Chambers of 544 Squadron who was interned in Sweden on 2 June 1944, and Flight Lieutenant J.L.H. Richards and Pilot Officer R.J. Barents both of 540 Squadron who were interned in Sweden on 10 August 1944, are now all back in the United Kingdom and have been classified as safe.

2 September 1944   544 Squadron

Flying Officer H. Woods and Flight Sergeant P. Bullimore took-off in Mosquito IX MM233 at 0705 hours on an operations mission PR106 G2593 to Ruhland, Magdeburg, Hitzacker, Jütebog, Dresden, Liegnitz and Breslau but failed to return.

Harry Woods, RAFVR, s/n 139965. Died on 2 September 1944 and is buried in the Berlin 1939-1945 War Cemetery.

Philip Bullimore, RAFVR, s/n 1545776, age 22, son of Jesse and Lillian Bullimore of Manchester, husband of Florence Bullimore of Wythenshawe, Manchester. Died on 2 September 1944 and is buried in the Berlin 1939-1945 War Cemetery.

6 September 1944   540 Squadron

Squadron Leader J.G. Fleming and Flying Officer H. Clark in Mosquito XVI MM300 took-off at 1100 hours for the Munich area but failed to return.

James Grant Fleming DFC, s/n 40380. Died on 6 September 1944 and is buried in the Rheinberg War Cemetery, Germany.

Harold Clark, RAFVR, s/n 141851, age 27, son of Daniel and Nellie Clark, husband of Joyce Edwina Clark of Frecheville, Sheffield. Died on 6 September 1944 and is buried in the Rheinberg War Cemetery, Germany.

9 September 1944   **RAF Station Benson**

Halifax VII NP681 of 426 Squadron crashed today at Wallingford. The pilot, Flying Officer J.A. Wilding, and flight engineer, Sergeant J.F. Andrew, were both killed, but the remaining five members of the crew successfully baled out. The aircraft was completely destroyed; bombs which were on board exploded on impact.

John Archibald Wilding, RCAF, s/n J/27908, age 23, son of Archibald and Rachel Wilding (née Hullock) of New York City, USA. Buried at Brookwood Military Cemetery.

John Francis Andrew, MiD, RAFVR, s/n 1199065, age 22, son of John and Ethel Andrew of Abermule, Wales. Buried in Kerry Cemetery.

14 September 1944   **540 Squadron**

Flying Officer H.P. Moylan and Flight Sergeant W.R. Morrell in Mosquito IX LR406 took-off at 1000 hours for the Leipzig area but failed to return.

Hilary Patrick Moylan, RAAF, s/n 403640, age 31, son of James and Maude Moylan; husband of Louise Moylan of Rose Bay, NSW, Australia. Died on 14 September 1944 and is buried in Hanover War Cemetery, Germany.

William Robert Morrell, RAFVR, s/n 1578889, son of William and Constance Morrell of Forest Fields, Nottinghamshire. Died on 14 September 1944 and is buried in Hanover War Cemetery, Germany.

14 September 1944   **544 Squadron**

Flight Lieutenant E.R. Jones and Flight Sergeant D.A.E. Parry in Mosquito XVI NS633 took-off for Königsberg, Gdynia, Danzig, Marienburg and Gleiwitz but failed to return.

Eric Reginald Jones, RAFVR, s/n 68781, age 30, son of George and Florence Jones of Green Street Green, Kent. Died on 14 September 1944 and is commemorated on the Runnymede Memorial.

Flight Sergeant D.A.E. Parry, s/n 1577455, was captured and became a prisoner of war, number 939, at Stalag Luft VII.

18 September 1944   **544 Squadron**

Flying Officer G.C.D. Hunter DFC and Flying Officer J. Fielden DFC in Mosquito IX MM231 took-off on a mission to Hamburg, Lübeck, Hitzacker and Parchim but failed to return.

Geoffrey Colin Devas Hunter DFC, s/n 126596, age 25, son of Lieutenant Colonel R. Devas Hunter DSO and Vixen Hunter of Walmer, Deal, Kent. Died on 18 September 1944 and is buried in the Berlin 1939-1945 War Cemetery.

John Fielden DFC, RAFVR, s/n 141154. Died on 18 September 1944 and is buried in the Berlin 1939-1945 War Cemetery.

20 September 1944   **RAF Station Benson**

An investigation was ordered into the loss of kit by Flight Sergeant J.F. Meech. Value of the kit was £6-2s-3d and it was lost on posting to this unit. Flying Officer A.E. Cooper has been appointed investigating officer.

27 September 1944   **RAF Station Benson**

There was an explosion in the Officers' Mess kitchen at Benson when a hot water boiler blew up at 1220 hours. Two civilians of the electrical contractors, Mr F.G. Alden and Mr A.R. Dew, were fatally injured.

28 September 1944   **541 Squadron**

Flight Lieutenant D. McCuaig in Spitfire PR XI PL904 took-off at 1305 hours on a sortie to Bremen but failed to return.

Duncan Kennedy McCuaig DFC, RAFVR, s/n 67629, age 24, son of Norman and Bertha McCuaig, husband of Olwen McCuaig of Dunblane, Perthshire. Died on 28 September 1944 and is buried at Sage War Cemetery, Germany.

5 October 1944   **542 Squadron**

Flight Lieutenant D. Rutherford in Spitfire PR X PA945 took-off at 1010 hours on a sortie to Bremen, Hanover and Hamburg but failed to return.

Flight Lieutenant D. Rutherford, s/n 65589, in Spitfire PA945 of 542 Squadron was captured and became a prisoner of war, number and camp unknown.

1944

13 October 1944   **RAF Station Benson**

The first known landing of the DH Reaction Jet aircraft was at Benson. The test pilot was Mr Geoffrey Pike. The aircraft took-off again after experts had worked on it for two hours.

17 October 1944   **RAF Station Benson**

A detachment of 540 Squadron proceeded to RAF Station Dyce for a one month stay. The complete party went by air with three Mosquitos and one Hudson. The detachment is to be responsible for PR in Norway.

27 October 1944   **540 Squadron**

Flying Officer K.R. Holland and Flying Officer G.J. Bloomfield in Mosquito PR XVI NS654 took-off on an operational sortie but failed to return.

Keith Ross Holland, RAAF, s/n 410234/ age 22, son of Herbert and Ada Holland of Mildura, Victoria, Australia. Died on 27 October 1944 and is buried in Heverlee War Cemetery, Belgium.

Geoffrey John Bloomfield, RAFVR, s/n 151271, age 22, son of Robert and Gertrude Bloomfield of Wallasey, Cheshire. Died on 27 October 1944 and is buried in Heverlee War Cemetery, Belgium.

11 November 1944   **540 Squadron**

Flight Lieutenant M.S. Lumsden and Flying Officer R.G. Metcalf in Mosquito PR XVI MM351 took-off at 1300 hours for the Minden, Herford and Paderborn area but failed to return.

Miller Stamford Lumsden, s/n 47832, age 27, son of Miller and Margaret Lumsden of Dulwich, London; husband of Dorothie Lumsden. Died on 11 November 1944 and is buried in Sage War Cemetery, Germany.

Ralph Gilbert Metcalf, RAFVR, s/n 145030, age 32, son of Ralph and Gertrude Metcalf, husband of Margaret Metcalf of Winchmore Hill, Middlesex. Died on 11 November 1944 and is buried in Sage War Cemetery, Germany.

16 November 1944   **RAF Station Benson**

Thirty-nine Liberators of the 8th USAAF landed due to weather conditions at their own base after bombing the Aachen area. No casualties; all the aircraft landed within 19 minutes. Thirty-six left on 18 November 1944. The remaining three with defects left within four days.

27 November 1944   542 Squadron

Flight Lieutenant G.R. Crakanthorp DFC in Spitfire PR XI PL906 took-off at 0920 hours on sortie Oil Jobs 5, 6, 12, 17, 386 and D/A of Munich area but failed to return. It is not known yet what happened to the pilot but that area is known to be one of the main areas where enemy jet fighters operate and has been taken over by Spitfire Squadrons from the Mosquitos for that reason after they had several losses and interceptions there.

Flight Lieutenant G.R. Crakanthorp, s/n 67057, was captured and became a prisoner of war, number and camp unknown.

29 November 1944   541 Squadron

Flying Officer J. Rowbotham in Spitfire XI PL887 was observed to have dived into the sea at Bradwell Bay and was killed.

John Neville Rowbotham, RAFVR, s/n 160133, age 23, son of Captain Victor S. Rowbotham, formerly RFC, and Coralie A. Rowbotham of Umberleigh, Devon. Died on 29 November 1944 and is buried in Combe Martin (St Peter) Churchyard.

5 December 1944   541 Squadron

Flying Officer W.S. Griffiths in Spitfire XI PL882 took-off at 1028 hours on sortie No. G3749 to the Cologne and Düsseldorf areas but failed to return.

William Stanwell Griffiths, RAFVR, s/n 170418, age 28, son of Cornelius and Kate Griffiths, husband of Margaret Griffiths of Solihull, Warwickshire. Died on 5 December 1944 and is buried in Jonkerbos War Cemetery, Holland.

18 December 1944   RAF Station Benson

Eighteen Liberators of the 8th USAAF landed due to weather conditions at their base. There were no casualties.

24 December 1944   **541 Squadron**

Flight Lieutenant N.P. Whaley in Spitfire XI PL919 took-off at 1055 hours on sortie No. G3908 to the Trier area but failed to return.

Noel Patrick Whaley DFC, RNZAF, s/n 412773, age 24, son of Edward and Florence Whaley (née Patterson) of Auckland, New Zealand. Died on 24 December 1944 and is buried in Hotton War Cemetery, Belgium.

24-30 December 1944   **RAF Station Benson**

Operations were diverted to Tangmere due to weather conditions at Benson.

29 December 1944   **544 Squadron**

Flight Lieutenant O.P. Olsen DFC and Flight Lieutenant A.M. Crow in Mosquito XVI NS791, took-off at 1015 hours to Hanover and Stendal but failed to return.

Since there appears to be no record of the death or imprisonment of Flight Lieutenant Olsen, a New Zealander, it is likely that he survived, escaped capture and returned to the United Kingdom.

Arthur Maurice Crow DSO, DFM, RAFVR, s/n 116137. Died on 29 December 1944 and is buried in Hanover War Cemetery, Germany.

RAF Station Benson – 541 Squadron Dispersal.

1945

1 January 1945   541 Squadron
Flying Officer D. Pollard in Spitfire XI PL889 took-off at 1010 hours on sortie No. G4022 to the Hamburg area but failed to return.

Douglas Pollard DFC, RAFVR, s/n 150050, age 23, son of Frederick and Nellie Pollard, husband of Peggy Pollard of Cambridge. Died on 1 January 1945 and is buried in Hamburg Ohlsdorf Cemetery.

6 January 1945   542 Squadron
Flying Officer L.G. Roberts in Spitfire XIX RM632 took-off at 1208 hours on a sortie to south-east of the Ruhr; the pilot baled out over the North Sea.

Leslie Glyn Roberts, RCAF, s/n J/19302, age 21, son of Dr Henry Charles Roberts MB, ChB and Kathleen Roberts of Oxton, Birkenhead. Died on 6 January 1945 and is commemorated on the Runnymede Memorial.

8 January 1945   542 Squadron
Flying Officer Durbridge DFM and Flight Sergeant K.J.H. Nichol carried out a local photography exercise of the new airfield at Heathrow.

9 January 1945   541 Squadron
Flight Lieutenant J.F.V. Puysseleyr in Spitfire X MD197 crashed in a snow storm near Watford at 1318 hours.

31 January – 20 February 1945
Operation Haycock

There was a requirement in connection with Operation Argonaut for the carrying of diplomatic mail between this country and the various destinations of the Argonaut conference. This requirement was made by No. 544 PR Squadron, of No. 106 PR Group, and entailed high level carrier flights between Benson and Malta, Benson and the Crimea, Benson and Athens and Benson and Cairo. Throughout the operation normal PR Mosquitos XVI were used, carrying 50 gallon drop tanks and with all photographic equipment removed. All crews of the Squadron took part in the operation on a normal roster and no special crews were used on any particular day.

544 Squadron couriers for Operation Haycock.

22 February 1945 — RAF Station Benson

First of two new Mosquitos received. Mosquito PR 34 differs from PR XVI as per following main features – Merlin 113 and 114 S.U. injection pumps, fuel tank protective coverings and armour plate deleted to save weight; bomb bay fuel tank increased by 180 gallons and a maximum range of more than 3,000 miles.

2 March 1945 — 540 Squadron

Final operational flight by 540 Squadron carried out today by PR IX Mosquito LR426.

3 March 1945 — 541 Squadron

Flying Officer W.G. Brooks in Spitfire XI PM148 took-off at 0820 hours on sortie No. G4624 to Bohlenlutzendorf and Rositz for D/A but failed to return.

William Gwynfryn Brooks, RAFVR, s/n 176857, age 27, son of William and Ann Brooks. Died on 3 March 1945 and is buried in the Berlin 1939-1945 War Cemetery.

4 March 1945 — 541 Squadron

Flight Lieutenant L.H. Scargill in Spitfire XIX RM627 took-off at 1042 hours on D/A sortie No. G4647 to Bielefeld but failed to return.

Since there appears to be no record of the death or imprisonment of Flight Lieutenant Scargill it is likely that he survived, escaped capture and returned to the United Kingdom.

9 March 1945 — 541 Squadron

Flight Lieutenant G. Platts in Spitfire XIX RM631 took-off at 0956 hours on sortie No. G4691 to Wesendorf, Dedelsdorf, Fassberg, Kohlenbissen, Celle, Hustedt and Musberg but failed to return.

George Platts DFC, RAFVR, s/n 137655. Died on 9 March 1945 and is commemorated on the Runnymede Memorial.

13 March 1945 — RAF Station Benson

Lancaster I N6263 of 150 Squadron crashed at Watlington. The wireless operator Sergeant J.H. Taylor was killed; the remainder of the crew baled out and sustained slight injuries and shock.

Jack Hugh Taylor, RAFVR, s/n 1336991, age 35, son of Abraham and Nellie Taylor, husband of Amy Taylor of Gillingham, Kent. Died on 13 March 1945 and is buried in Gillingham (Woodlands) Cemetery.

14 March 1945 — 541 Squadron

Lieutenant G.F. Godden (SAAF), in Mustang XI FB182 on D/A sortie G4808 to Arnsberg, failed to return.

Since there appears to be no record of the death or imprisonment of Lieutenant Godden, it is likely that he survived, escaped capture and returned to the United Kingdom.

19 March 1945 — 541 Squadron

Flight Lieutenant B.K. Fuge in Spitfire XI PC857 took-off at 1504 hours on sortie G4931 to Neustadt, Oranienburg, Hanover, Musberg, Reinsehlen, Perleberg and Lüneburg but failed to return.

Brian Kenneth Levinge Fuge, s/n 41394, age 28, son of T.L. and Francis Fuge, husband of Olive Fuge of Bangor, Co. Down. Died on 19 March 1945 and is commemorated on the Runnymede Memorial.

21 March 1945 — 541 Squadron

Flying Officer F.P. Adlam (NZAF) in Spitfire XIX RM635 took-off at 1745 hours on sortie No. G4951 but crashed at East Grinstead and was killed.

Frank Percival Adlam, RNZAF, s/n 424403/ age 29, son of Ernest and Jessie Adlam of Stratford, Taranaki, New Zealand, husband of Phyllis Adlam of Midhurst, Taranaki, New Zealand. Buried in Brookwood Military Cemetery.

22 March 1945 — 544 Squadron

Squadron Leader F.L. Dodd and Pilot Officer L. Hill in Mosquito XVI NS637 on an operations sortie to Tromsø to look at the *Tirpitz*, carried out the longest sortie of the war – 10½ hours.

Flight Lieutenant J. Robson (left) and Flying Officer F. Adlam with a Spitfire of 541 Squadron. [See 21 March 1945]

The capsized German battleship *Tirpitz* near Tromsø, Norway. [See 22 March 1945]

25 March 1945 — 544 Squadron

Flight Lieutenant S.M. Mackay and Flying Officer A.S. Lobban in Mosquito XVI RF971 took-off at 1130 hours to Swinemünde and Stettin but failed to return.

Since there appear to be no records of the death or imprisonment of these crew members, it is likely that they both survived, escaped capture and returned to the United Kingdom.

29 March 1945 — 544 Squadron

Flight Lieutenant J.B. Sparkes and Flight Sergeant H. Thompson in Mosquito XVI NS814 force landed at Wallingford. The pilot was slightly injured.

30 March 1945 — 544 Squadron

Flying Officer R.M. Hays and Acting Flight Lieutenant D. South in Mosquito XVI NS396 took-off at 1430 hours on an operations sortie to Denmark and the Baltic. The aircraft crashed at Wallingford and both of the crew were killed.

Raymond Morris Hays, RCAF, s/n J/88928, age 31, son of Mr & Mrs Lorenzo D. Hays, husband of Beatrice Hays of Chester-le-Street, Co. Durham. Died on 30 March 1945 and is buried in Oxford (Botley) Cemetery.

Donald South, RAFVR, s/n 151174, age 35, son of James and Emily South, husband of Irene South of Kingsbury, Middlesex. Died on 30 March 1945 and is buried in Oxford (Botley) Cemetery.

1 April 1945 — RAF Station Benson

Air Commodore D.J. Waghorn AFC AOC No. 106 PR Group, crashed at Boscombe Down in Spitfire PS831 and was killed.

David John Waghorn CBE, AFC, age 37, son of John and Ada Waghorn, husband of Stella Waghorn of Upper Woodford, Wiltshire. Died on 1 April 1945 and is commemorated at Oxford Crematorium.

1 April 1945   RAF Station Benson

Mosquito XVI MM328 of PRDU Benson crashed at RAF Station Southrop while carrying out a test flight of the GEC Auto Pilot. The pilot Flight Lieutenant J.L.H. Richards and passenger Flying Officer W.E. Robinson, electrical officer, were both killed.

John Leicester Hazell Richards DFC (US), s/n 47726, age 27, son of John and Gladys Richards, husband of June Richards of Kings Ripton, Huntingdon. Died on 1 April 1945 and is buried in Oxford (Botley) Cemetery.

William Ernest Robinson, RAFVR, s/n 134972, age 26, son of William and Edith Robinson, husband of Margaret Robinson of Liverpool. Died on 1 April 1945 and is buried in Liverpool (Toxteth Park) Cemetery.

5 April 1945   RAF Station Benson

The funeral took place today of the late Air Commodore Waghorn. The funeral procession left RAF Station Benson at 1000 hours and proceeded to the Oxford road via the perimeter track from whence the remainder of the journey was made by road to Oxford Crematorium.

5 April 1945   RAF Station Benson

Lancaster I RF150 of 424 Squadron crashed at Widdington Park near High Wycombe. The crew of seven, all of the RCAF, were killed.

12 April 1945   544 Squadron

Flight Lieutenant E.V. Warwick and Pilot Officer H.A. Stapleton in Mosquito XVI took-off at 1110 hours originally in RG133 but returned at 1320 hours due to non feed of drop tanks. At 1355 hours they took-off again in NS500 on a mission to Swinemünde, Kaiser Fahrt Canal, Nekso, Ronne, Pasewalk and Tonder but failed to return.

Edmund Vernon Warwick, RAFVR, s/n 117037, age 23, son of Horace and Florence Warwick of Edgware, Middlesex. Died on 12 April 1945 and is commemorated on the Runnymede Memorial.

Harold Arthur Stapleton, RAFVR, s/n 191707, age 22, son of Frederick and Florence Stapleton of Fishponds, Gloucestershire. Died on 12 April 1945 and is commemorated on the Runnymede Memorial.

5 May 1945 **544 Squadron**

The Squadron carried out its final mission today with Mosquito MM276.

8 May 1945 **RAF Station Benson**

RAF Station Benson celebrates VE day.

Appendix I

Summary of Aircraft Losses

Unit	A/C	FTR	C	F/L	C/L
RAF Station Benson	Tiger Moth	-	1	-	-
52 Squadron	Battle	-	5	3	-
63 Squadron	Mustang	1	-	-	-
12 OTU	Wellington	-	2	-	-
PRU	Spitfire	11	3	3	-
140 Squadron	Spitfire	4	5	1	-
170 Squadron	Mustang	-	-	1	-
No. 1 PRU	Mosquito	3	1	-	-
No. 1 PRU	Spitfire	30	12	-	-
No. 1 PRU Wick	Spitfire	8	-	-	-
No. 1 PRU Wick	Mosquito	1	-	-	-
No. 1 PRU St Eval	Spitfire	3	2	-	-
No. 1 PRU Leuchars	Mosquito	2	-	-	-
Russian Detachment	Spitfire	1	-	-	-
540 Squadron	Mosquito	24	-	3	-
540 Squadron Leuchars	Mosquito	3	4	1	-
540 Squadron Gibraltar	Mosquito	1	-	-	-
540 Squadron	Spitfire	1	-	1	-
541 Squadron	Spitfire	19	5	5	3
541 Squadron	Mustang	1	-	-	-
541 Squadron Leuchars	Spitfire	1	-	-	-
541 Squadron Gibraltar	Spitfire	-	-	2	-
542 Squadron	Spitfire	14	5	1	1
543 Squadron	Spitfire	1	1	1	-
543 Squadron Mount Farm	Spitfire	1	-	-	-
543 Squadron St Eval	Spitfire	2	-	-	-
544 Squadron	Tiger Moth	-	-	1	-
544 Squadron	Mosquito	11	6	2	-
544 Squadron Gibraltar	Spitfire	2	-	-	-

Appendix I

544 Squadron Gibraltar	Mosquito	1	-	-	-
544 Squadron Leuchars	Mosquito	1	1	-	-
PRDU Benson	Mosquito	-	1	-	-
	Totals	147	54	25	4

A/C = Aircraft
FTR = Failed to return
C = Crashed
F/L = Force Landed
C/L = Crash Landed

Appendix II

No. 8 (Coastal) Operational Training Unit

No. 8 OTU came into being at Fraserburgh on 18 May 1942 as part of 17 Group. It was formed by a merger of the Operational Training Flight of No. 1 PRU and the PRU Conversion Flight of No. 3 School of General Reconnaissance. Its main function was to train Spitfire pilots for a photographic reconnaissance role but this expanded to include Mosquito crews in November 1942. At the end of January 1943 it moved to Dyce. In July 1943 the command changed from 17 Group to 16 Group when it was transferred to No. 106 (PR) Wing. It moved briefly to Haverfordwest (17 Group) and then went to Mount Farm in June 1945 as part of the newly formed No. 106 (PR) Group. It remained there for a year before moving to Chalgrove for three months and then to Benson in October 1946, where it stayed until it was disbanded on 31 July 1947.

Casualties and incidents from No. 8 OTU; a feeder unit to PRU, at Fraserburgh

21 May 1942
Wing Commander Lord M.A. Douglas-Hamilton took command of the station.

11 June 1942
Sergeant Renshaw was picked up from the sea out of Spitfire AR241 which sank.

30 June 1942

Pilot Officer W.T. Vlasto, flying Spitfire X4715 crashed into the sea. His body was recovered on 1 July.

William Theodore Vlasto, RAFVR, s/n 115917, age 22, son of Ivan and Florence Vlasto of Stockton Heath, Lancashire. Buried in Lossiemouth Burial Ground, Scotland. Pilot Officer Vlasto was a classical scholar at Jesus College, Cambridge.

29 July 1942

Sergeant W.L. McGinn and Sergeant H.J. Miller, both Canadians, were killed in a flying accident in Miles Master L8786.

Wilfred Lawrence McGinn, RCAF, s/n R/82408, age 24. Son of Mr & Mrs Denver McGinn of Iroquois, Ontario, Canada. Buried in Longside Cemetery, Scotland.

Hugh John Miller, RCAF, s/n R/94978, age 20. Son of Michael and Eretta Miller of Grimshaw, Alberta, Canada. Buried in Longside Cemetery, Scotland.

11 September 1942

Sergeant F.T. Martyn was killed in a crash at Montrose in Spitfire R6968.

Frederick Thomas Martyn, RNZAF, s/n 413875, age 21. Son of Frederick and Robina Martyn of Seaward Downs, Southland, New Zealand. Buried in Montrose (Sleepyhillock) Cemetery, Scotland.

1 October 1942

Pilot Officer P.A. Jupp took-off in Spitfire P9310 at 1400 hours for a high photography exercise in the Newcastle area but failed to return.

Philip Anthony Jupp, RAFVR, s/n 123126. Buried in Sage War Cemetery, Germany.

5 November 1942

Sergeant Harvey baled out of his Spitfire due to engine trouble. He was unhurt.

10 November 1942

Sergeant W.A. Jolly on a cross-country flight, in Spitfire X4437, hit a hill near to Edzell and was killed.

William Albert Jolly, RAFVR, s/n 1271932, age 22. Son of William and Nellie Jolly of Shoreditch. Buried in Highgate Cemetery.

5 January 1943

Flight Lieutenant A.M. Wodehouse in Spitfire X4599 failed to return from a training flight.

Arthur Miller Wodehouse, RAFVR, s/n 82168, age 34. Son of Arthur and Em Wodehouse of Barnes, Surrey. Commemorated on the Runnymede Memorial.

18 January 1943

Sergeant P.J. Miles (No. 10 course) in Spitfire III X4498 baled out at Dornie, Kyle of Lochalsh, due to engine failure. Due to insufficient height the parachute did not open and the pilot was killed.

Philip John Miles, s/n 657304, age 21. Son of Mr & Mrs P.J. Miles of Wood End, Tamworth-in-Arden. Buried in Yardley Wood (Christ Church) Churchyard.

22 January 1943

Sergeant F.J. Richardson in Spitfire PR VII X4333 stalled on approach to landing; the aircraft spun into the sea and the pilot was killed.

Frederick John Richardson, RAFVR, s/n 1237358, age 22. Son of William and Winifred Richardson of Great Barr, Birmingham. Buried in Cairnbulg and Inverallochy Burial Ground, Rathen, Scotland.

22 January 1943

Sergeant F.V. Mooney in Spitfire X4501 turned over in a field due to the engine cutting out. The pilot was injured.

27 January 1943

8 OTU moved to Dyce (17 Group) and Group Captain J.W. Colquhoun assumed command of the station from Lord M.A. Douglas-Hamilton.

27 February 1943

Sergeant A.W. Gardner in Spitfire BR651 failed to return from an exercise in the Belfast area.

Albert Walter Gardner, RAFVR, s/n 1387373, age 30. Son of Albert and Beatrice Gardner and husband of Joyce Gardner of Foulsham, Norfolk. The Commonwealth War Graves Commission shows Sergeant Gardner's date of death as being 6 March 1943. It is likely that this is the date his body was found, given the long distance between where he was last known to be and the place of his burial, Trondheim (Stavne) Cemetery, Norway.

13 May 1943

Pilot Officer R.J.F. Fiscalini in Spitfire X4334 crashed into the sea 3 miles north of Thurso. The pilot's body was recovered the next day.

Ronald James Fiscalini, RAAF, s/n 409535, age 23. Son of Martin and Evelyn Fiscalini and husband of Doris Fiscalini of Hurstbridge, Victoria, Australia. Buried in Olrig New Cemetery, Scotland.

16 May 1943

Pupil pilot, Pilot Officer J.D.M. McDonell in Spitfire X4326 crashed near to Fort William on a cross-country exercise and was killed.

John Donald McDonell, RCAF, s/n J/13408, age 21. Son of Mr & Mrs A.R. McDonell of Smithers, British Columbia, Canada. Buried in Inverness (Tomnahurich) Cemetery, Scotland.

21 May 1943

Sergeant Pilot L.A. Wearn in Spitfire X4839 failed to return from a cross-country exercise to the Darlington area. No trace of the aircraft or pilot was found.

Leslie Allan Wearn, RCAF, s/n R/127520, age 24. Son of Arthur and Helen Wearn of Claremont, Ontario, Canada. Commemorated on the Runnymede Memorial.

28 May 1943

Miles Master DM160 crashed and was written off. The pupil pilot, Sergeant Severn was uninjured.

28 May 1943

Spitfire BP926 was written off after crashing at Bardney near Lincoln. The pilot, Sergeant Hornsey, was unhurt.

31 May 1943

Pilot Officer H.V.C. Sheppard in Spitfire X4505 crashed east of Macmerry while on a cross-country exercise. The aircraft was wrecked and the pilot was killed.

Henry Valentine Charles Sheppard, RAAF, s/n 409755, age 20. Son of Henry and Teresa Sheppard of Benalla, Victoria, Australia. Buried in Haddington (St Martin's) New Burial Ground, Scotland.

19 June 1943

Sergeant J.E. Mosley crashed in Spitfire R7198 while on a cross-country exercise at Talisker, Isle of Skye. The aircraft was wrecked and the pilot was killed.

John Edwin Mosley, RAFVR, s/n 1467449, age 22. Son of John and Bertha Mosley of South Shore, Blackpool. Commemorated in Blackpool (Carleton) Crematorium, Poulton-Le-Fylde.

15 July 1943

Command change from 17 Group to 16 Group

25 July 1943

Flight Sergeant J.A. Davis in Spitfire R7059 crashed at Laurencekirk. The pilot was killed and the aircraft was written off.

John Ashby Davis, RAFVR, s/n 1384191, age 20. Son of Herbert and Margery Davis of Bournemouth, Hampshire. Buried in Brookwood Military Cemetery.

17 August 1943

Pupil pilot Sergeant G.E.R. Hornsey in Mosquito HJ895 crashed at Dyce and was killed; instructor Flying Officer George was badly injured. The aircraft was a complete write off.

George Edward Ronald Hornsey, RAFVR, of 544 Squadron, s/n 1256894, age 21. Son of George and Margaret Hornsey and husband of Mavis Hornsey. Buried in City of London Cemetery and Crematorium, Manor Park.

6 October 1943

Pilot Braathen and navigator Lieutenant N. Rohnes in Mosquito DK320 failed to return from a flight over the Orkneys. Later part of the aircraft was washed up near to Sullom Voe. No further details are known.

6 October 1943

Flight Sergeant C. Dickson in Spitfire AB124 was reported missing on a training flight. The aircraft crashed into the sea near to Coquet Island. No further details are known.

10 November 1943

Flight Lieutenant H.G.J. Coddington in Spitfire N3059 was reported missing from a training flight.

Hubert Geoffrey John Coddington, s/n 45331, age 24. Son of Arthur and Dorothy Coddington and husband of Yvonne Coddington. Commemorated on the Runnymede Memorial.

11 November 1943

Pilot Officer A.J.F. Symes, pilot, and Sergeant E. Lyon, navigator, in Mosquito DZ459, crashed two miles south of Thornaby. Both crew members were killed and the aircraft was written off.

Alan John Farquhar Symes, RCAF, s/n J/7617, age 22. Son of Alan and Margaret Symes and husband of Margaret Symes of Rockcliffe, Ontario, Canada. Buried in Thornaby-on-Tees Cemetery.

Edward Lyon, RAFVR, s/n 1433734, age 20. Son of Elizabeth Lyon of Lathom. Buried in Burscough Bridge (St John the Baptist) Churchyard, Ormskirk.

19 November 1943

Warrant Officer J.L. Kelly in Spitfire AR242 crashed into the sea. The aircraft was a complete write off and the pilot was reported missing.

John Lomer Kelly, RCAF, s/n R/82270, age 21. Son of John and Mary Kelly of Ottawa, Ontario, Canada. Commemorated on the Runnymede Memorial.

6 December 1943

Six Mosquitos undertook high level photography in the Shetlands and Hebrides.

Further high and low level photography was carried out by Mosquitos and Spitfires throughout the month.

15 December 1943

'A' Flight (Spitfire conversion) disbanded and all instructors absorbed into 'B' Flight which will, in future, operate all Spitfire aircraft of No. 8 OTU.

21 December 1943

No. 30 Course completed training after a two week extension and proceeded on leave prior to posting to Benson wef 28 December 1943. Of the nine crews posted in for the course, one crew was killed on 11 November 1943 and one crew transferred to No. 31 Course.

23 December 1943

Wing Commander E.C. Mesurier, DSO, DFC, MiD, Chief Instructor No. 8 (C) OTU and Aircraftman 1st Class L.F. Gough (F11A) were killed in an accident to Mosquito HJ964. The aircraft, which was undergoing an air test, crashed two miles north-east of RAF Station Dyce.

Eric Clive Le Mesurier, s/n **37883**, age 28. Son of Major and Mrs Le Mesurier of Weymouth. Buried in Radipole (St Ann) Churchyard Extension.

Lawrence Frederick Gough, RAFVR, s/n 1221770. Buried in Mansfield (Nottingham Road) Cemetery.

Appendix III

RAF Benson Station Commanders 1939-1945

March 1939	Group Captain R.T. Leather AFC
September 1939	Group Captain C.W. Mackay
May 1940	Group Captain W.H. Dunn DSC
September 1940	Group Captain G.F. Smylie DSC
August 1941	Group Captain J. Bussey
June 1943	Air Commodore J.N. Boothman AFC
July 1943	Group Captain W.B. Murray DFC
April 1944	Group Captain C.E. St J Beamish DFC
May 1945	Group Captain B.J.R. Roberts

Appendix IV

List of Honours and Awards to the officers and men of 106 (PR) Group 1939 – 1945

Distinguished Service Order

Squadron Leader D.M. Fairhurst
Squadron Leader G.E. Hughes
Squadron Leader J.R.H. Merifield
Squadron Leader J.H. Saffery
Squadron Leader G. Singlehurst
Squadron Leader D.W. Steventon

Flight Lieutenant R.L. Blythe
Flight Lieutenant A.M. Crow
Flight Lieutenant F.L. Dodd
Flight Lieutenant E.C. Le Mesurier
Flight Lieutenant P.H. Watts

Distinguished Flying Cross

Air Commodore J.N. Boothman

Squadron Leader W.R. Acott
Squadron Leader W.R. Assheton
Squadron Leader A.C. Graham
Squadron Leader R.A. Lenton
Squadron Leader N.H.E. Messervy

Flight Lieutenant G.K. Arnold
Flight Lieutenant K.F. Arnold
Flight Lieutenant J. Bendixson
Flight Lieutenant N.J. Bonnar

Flight Lieutenant J. Burfield
Flight Lieutenant L.E. Clark
Flight Lieutenant T.N. Clutterbuck
Flight Lieutenant P. Curbishley
Flight Lieutenant A.R. Cussons
Flight Lieutenant R.C. Cussons
Flight Lieutenant W.R. Donaghue
Flight Lieutenant K. Durbidge
Flight Lieutenant E.A. Fairhurst
Flight Lieutenant R.N. Foster
Flight Lieutenant D.R.M. Furniss
Flight Lieutenant A.R. Graham

APPENDIX IV   147

Flight Lieutenant W.N. Harris
Flight Lieutenant A.E. Hill
Flight Lieutenant R.J. Keefer
Flight Lieutenant E.G.C. Leatham
Flight Lieutenant E.D.L. Lee
Flight Lieutenant M.V. Longbottom
Flight Lieutenant A.M. Lott
Flight Lieutenant D.K. McCuaig
Flight Lieutenant B.J. McMaster
Flight Lieutenant J.R.H. Merifield
Flight Lieutenant E.C. Le Mesurier
Flight Lieutenant G.D. Milne
Flight Lieutenant A.P. Morgan
Flight Lieutenant W.J.G. Morgan
Flight Lieutenant R.H. Niven
Flight Lieutenant H.C.S. Powell
Flight Lieutenant P.T. Pratt
Flight Lieutenant J.F.V.R. de
          Puysseleyr
Flight Lieutenant H. Reeves
Flight Lieutenant V.A. Ricketts
Flight Lieutenant S.L. Ring
Flight Lieutenant F.A. Robinson
Flight Lieutenant D. Salwey
Flight Lieutenant E.G. Searle
Flight Lieutenant N.D. Sinclair
Flight Lieutenant G.B. Singlehurst
Flight Lieutenant J.H. Spires
Flight Lieutenant B.H.F. Templar
Flight Lieutenant G.E. Walker
Flight Lieutenant G. Watson
Flight Lieutenant J.A.M. Weatherill
Flight Lieutenant J.C. Webb
Flight Lieutenant H.N.G. Wheeler
Flight Lieutenant R.V. Whitehead
Flight Lieutenant G.W. Williams
Flight Lieutenant L.D. Wilson
Flight Lieutenant M.J.B. Young

Flying Officer M.B.C. Anderson
Flying Officer K.H. Bailey
Flying Officer J.H.L. Blaunt
Flying Officer J.R. Brew
Flying Officer R.M. Campbell
Flying Officer G.P. Christie
Flying Officer G.R. Crakanthorp
Flying Officer A.J.W. Crofton

Flying Officer S.G. Dale
Flying Officer J. Dearden
Flying Officer J.H. Dickson
Flying Officer E. Efford
Flying Officer J. Fielden
Flying Officer F.G. Fray
Flying Officer G.T.V. Graxton
Flying Officer E.H. Grennan
Flying Officer D. Hill
Flying Officer M.D.S. Hood
Flying Officer G.E. Hughes
Flying Officer G.C.D. Hunter
Flying Officer J.D. Ibbotson
Flying Officer R.F. Leavitt
Flying Officer R.E. Mackie
Flying Officer L. McMillan
Flying Officer J. Miles
Flying Officer S.J. Millon
Flying Officer T.W. Osborne
Flying Officer W. Panton
Flying Officer G.W. Puttick
Flying Officer H.J. Richardson
Flying Officer P. Riches
Flying Officer J.F. Samson
Flying Officer G.D. Scott
Flying Officer J.H. Shelmerdine
Flying Officer A.G. Shingles
Flying Officer E.J. Sillitoe
Flying Officer D.W. Steventon
Flying Officer A. Stewart
Flying Officer A.L. Taylor
Flying Officer T.P. Turnbull
Flying Officer P.H. Watts
Flying Officer S.G. Wise
Flying Officer Z. Wysiekierski

Pilot Officer R.L.C. Blythe
Pilot Officer J.A.D. Deighton
Pilot Officer J.T. Leach
Pilot Officer J.M.K. Little
Pilot Officer A. McLeod
Pilot Officer M.A. Mortimer
Pilot Officer J.D. Muir
Pilot Officer W. Nelson
Pilot Officer W.J. White

Warrant Officer G. Macarthur
Warrant Officer R.E. Somervaille
Warrant Officer F.H. Moseley

Captain G.A.D. Williams

Bars to Distinguished Flying Cross

Wing Commander J.H. Merifield
Wing Commander D.W. Steventon
Wing Commander M.J.B. Yany

Squadron Leader M.D.S. Hood
Squadron Leader G.E. Hughes
Squadron Leader A.T. Leaning

Flight Lieutenant G.R. Crakanthorp
Flight Lieutenant R.F.C. Garvey
Flight Lieutenant A.E. Hill
Flight Lieutenant A.L. Taylor (2nd bar)

Distinguished Flying Medal

Sergeant G.B. Lukhmanoff
Sergeant W. Morgan

Sergeant J.A.M. Reid
Sergeant R.F. Walker

British Empire Medal

Wing Commander F.S. Cotton

Squadron Leader T.W. Ellcock

Flight Lieutenant D.P. Bamber

Pilot Officer A.H.R. Taylor
Pilot Officer W.R. Owen

Sergeant D.S. Upstone

Air Force Cross

Flying Officer N.J. Bonnar

Order of the British Empire

Squadron Leader Q.C. Craig

Appendix IV

Order of the Bath

Air Commodore J.N. Boothman

Foreign Honours and Awards

Air Medal USA

Wing Commander S.L. Ring

Squadron Leader D.W. Steventon

Flying Officer D. Wilson
Flying Officer D.G. Scott
Flying Officer J. Dearden

Flying Officer W.M.O. Jones
Flying Officer G. Platts
Flying Officer L. McMillan

Pilot Officer J.R. Miles

Virtute Militaire Poland

Flying Officer Z. Wysiekierski

Croix de Guerre Belgium

Flying Officer J.F.V.R. de Puysseleyr
Pilot Officer A.J.E. Cantillion

Order of Patriotic War (1st Degree) Russia

Squadron Leader F.A. Robinson

Medal for Distinguished Battle Service Russia

Flying Officer J.H. Dixon
Flying Officer B.K. Kenwright

Total Mentioned in Dispatches

132

Left: Flying Officer N.J. Bonnar. [See pages 146 & 148]

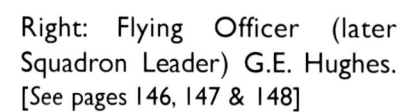

Right: Flying Officer (later Squadron Leader) G.E. Hughes. [See pages 146, 147 & 148]

Below: Flight Lieutenant P.H. Watts [left] after receiving his DSO at Buckingham Palace. [See pages 146 & 147]

Buckingham Palace Feb. 17th. 1942.

Appendix V

Brief History of Photographic Reconnaissance since 1939

This history, written in two parts and originally classified 'Secret', was issued by Headquarters No. 106 (PR) Group in October 1944. Curiously it fails to mention the move of the Photographic Reconnaissance Unit from Heston to RAF Station Benson at the end of 1940.

Part One

By the end of 1918 the volume of reconnaissance had reached immense proportions, so much so that during the last year of the war no less than 1,000,000 prints were supplied per month to the army in the field. However, by the time that war broke out again in 1939 most of the lessons learnt had been forgotten and the RAF was faced with building up an organization almost ab initio.

2. It was however a very different problem that had to be faced from that of the last war. For instance, then photography was largely tactical and confined to the main battle areas, whereas in this war the range of modern aircraft opened up potentially most areas occupied by the enemy. Thus there was no precedent upon which to base the organization; there was little data from which the results which were to be achieved could be forecast and all that existed was a knowledge that in the last war a great deal had been obtained from air photographs.

3. Before the war it had, of course, been appreciated that photography would be required but no special Photographic

Reconnaissance unit had been visualized. It was realized that the army would require photography first of all strategically and later, as operations developed, tactically. To meet this requirement certain army cooperation squadrons were equipped with Blenheims for the long range photographic work and others with Lysanders for short range reconnaissance. Accordingly when war broke out in 1939 a number of these squadrons moved to France with the Air Component.

4. Meanwhile, it was also realized that the Air Force would require photography first of all for target location and later for damage assessment after the attack. It was therefore laid down as one of the functions of any aircraft in any bomber squadron that they might be required to undertake photographic reconnaissance from time to time, although on the whole, such jobs would naturally have fallen to the 1st of the day bombers of No. 2 Group.

5. The first two months of war quickly proved that an unescorted Blenheim flying at 15/20,000 feet deep in enemy territory by day had little chance of arrival, particularly as those days suitable for photography were obviously those mainly lacking in cloud cover. Portions of the Siegfried line were certainly photographed from France at a cost, but photography of the Ruhr proved to be almost impossible. It was therefore clear that some new technique was required.

6. The obvious answer to the difficulty was to evolve an aircraft which could fly sufficiently fast and sufficiently high to avoid interception. RAE Farnborough were therefore charged with the responsibility of producing such an aircraft and selected the Spitfire for their experiments. The latter was then making its first appearance in any quantity and was the only aircraft available possessing the necessary performance.

7. The first step consisted of lightening the aircraft so that long range tanks and cameras could be fitted. This was done by removing the armament. The cameras then had to be fitted. At that time virtually the only camera available in the RAF was the standard F.24. The whole theory of photographic reconnaissance was based on the expectation that

photographs would be obtained from 15/20,000 feet and therefore the existing focal length of the lenses with which the F.24 was equipped were designed to give an adequate scale of photography for interpretation from these heights and not from heights over 30,000 feet. The cameras available for installation were therefore F.24s with 5 inch or 8 inch focal length lenses. The easiest place to install the cameras was in the wings and therefore the original two Spitfires sent to RAE had a vertical 5 inch F.24 camera mounted in each wing.

8. Initial tests proved satisfactory and at the end of November 1939 these two Spitfires were moved to Heston where they became operational under the name of the 'Heston Special Flight'. The next stage was to try out the theory in practice and it obviously presented many new problems. For instance there was the question as to how the pilot could stand up to 3 or 4 hours at 34,000 feet and there was no other previous experience upon which to base this. Oxygen apparatus was not as efficient as it is today. There was the question of navigation. Hitherto all photography had been done in a bomber with a navigator and observer to guide the pilot during his runs across the target. This new idea meant that the pilot had to do everything and since from his Spitfire he could not see the ground details below him, was compelled to adopt a new technique for his navigation, flying on a track 12 miles to port.

9. Then there was the question of how the camera would behave under the conditions of extreme cold which would be encountered. One of the earliest problems was that the batteries which operated the camera froze. This was got over by moving them nearer the engine. Then, as anticipated, the cameras broke down but there was seldom a completely nil result since there was a camera in each wing both covering the same ground. If one broke down usually the other worked. However the camera trouble was finally got over by blowing hot air from the exhaust onto them.

10. Once the reliability of the camera had been assured the next stage was to make both cameras productive by tilting

them both outwards a little from the vertical, so that each covered different areas with a common overlap of about 10 per cent down the centre. This enabled double the area to be covered on each flight.

Part Two

The first flight of the Heston Special Flight was made on 18 November 1939 and was intended to cover Aachen. Not unnaturally the anticipated difficulties of navigating a Spitfire over the right area proved well founded for the tricks had yet to be learnt and the result of this first effort was some photographs of Eupen on the Belgian side of the frontier. Nothing further was obtained until 21 December 1939 when two flights were made; a third flight was made on 22 December 1939 and between these three sorties a large part of the Siegfried Line between Saarbrücken and Aachen was covered. These three flights went a long way towards proving that an effective instrument had been evolved but the final proof was given when, on 2 March 1940, the 10th flight, the whole of the Ruhr was photographed during one sortie.

2. A serious problem now arose. Operational experience had certainly proved that the method was right and that photographs could and were being obtained. But the camera being used was not designed to obtain photographs at such heights. The result was that the photographs produced were of minute scale, in fact no less than 1/80,000, each one covering about 40 square miles of country on a negative 5 inches by 5 inches. Those faced with the problem of interpreting the photographs were therefore presented with a medium only capable of giving very limited results. Inevitably this state of affairs had to continue until such a time as new photographic equipment with longer focal length lenses could be procured. In fact it was early in April 1940 before the first 20 inch focal length camera was made available and very many months before they came into general use. These longer focal length cameras of course provided a new problem since they were too large to fit into

the wing and space had therefore to be found for them immediately behind the pilot.

3. Once the idea of a special high flying photographic reconnaissance unit had been established the organization developed rapidly. Its name was first changed from Heston Special Flight to No. 2 Camouflage Unit. The latter was however short lived and by March 1940 it had become the Photographic Development Unit (PDU). Small numbers of Spitfires became available each month and by February 1940 it was found possible to send the first flight of two Spitfires to Lille in France, from where they could fulfil BEF requirements. During this time much was also done to improve the aircraft themselves. Since they were always kept under cover camouflage on the ground was unnecessary. They were therefore 'cleaned up' as far as possible, painted blue so that they would disappear visually at height and polished to give them increased speed.

4. As the unit expanded further flights were sent to France where they operated as 212 Squadron, the flights being based initially at Lille, Nancy and the south of France. From Nancy they operated over south Germany dealing mainly with French requests while from the south of France, sometimes using Corsica for refuelling, they operated over Italy. Later when the Germans broke through, the flights at Lille and Nancy were withdrawn to Meaux (east of Paris) which was the site of the French central interpretation unit and which was also conveniently located for close contact with the FAEF at Coulomniers.

5. Meanwhile in England at Heston further development continued and the range and performance of the Photographic Reconnaissance Spitfires was improved. Finally on 7 April 1940 it was found possible to send an aircraft to Kiel for the first time. The resulting sortie studied now in the light of present knowledge is of the greatest interest. The port shows great activity, convoys are sailing out and there are over 60 Ju52s on the aerodrome. Unfortunately the port had never been photographed before so that the small handful of officers who had been collected

together and told to interpret such photographs as should be obtained from time to time, had no basis for comparison. The reputation of Kiel as the main German Naval Base was such that they would hardly have been surprised at anything which they had seen. The result was that although they reported what they saw, they made no remark that things were a little unusual and certainly had no idea that they had witnessed the departure of invading German forces for Norway. As for the 60 Ju52s on the aerodrome the interpreters had yet to learn the art of naming aircraft and their presence was not reported until a post-mortem was made a year later. There is little doubt that had the photographic reconnaissance unit been developed when war broke out and obtained from the start regular photography of the focal points of Germany, the invasion of Norway would have been forecast, provided always that interpreters properly trained in their duties had also been available from the outset.

6. With the fall of France the whole character of photographic reconnaissance changed and from a little used experiment it became an essential reality. Until the collapse, intelligence concerning the enemy from sources other than photographic reconnaissance seemed adequate to meet most needs and comparatively little attention was paid to the development of photography and interpretation. With the collapse however, followed complete disorganization of these other sources, coupled with loss of all the information from the French 2nd Bureau organization and at the same time occupation by the enemy of large areas for which little in the way of intelligence organization had been established. Perforce therefore it was necessary to turn to photographic reconnaissance and development with the utmost speed.

7. It was about this time that PDU altered its name and became No. 1 PRU (Photographic Reconnaissance Unit). It was still small, far too small to meet the enormous calls to be made on it, and Spitfires were still slow in coming along in the face of the pressing demands of Fighter Command who were preparing for the Battle of Britain. Reconnaissance had therefore to be confined to the coastal ports which were at

any rate the focal points through which the invasion must come. In this way these ports were very closely watched although at the expense of the aerodrome behind them, the marshalling yards that fed them, but, most serious of all, at the expense of damage assessment for Bomber Command. The latter was a necessary evil but an unfortunate one since Bomber Command had been attacking the Ruhr almost nightly for about three months without ever receiving a photograph from which the results could be judged. It was not until such photographs were available that a study could be made of the results achieved and thus important decisions made on the effectiveness of the type of bomb which was being used, and the tactics we were employing. Nor was it appreciated until extensive inland photographic cover had been obtained to what extent the enemy were using decoy fire sites to draw off the main weight of our attack.

8. The final result was that a new PRU known as No. 3 PRU was formed with the express purpose of obtaining the photography required by Bomber Command. It achieved its purpose but inevitably caused duplication of effort which was finally crowned when two aircraft from No. 1 and No. 3 PRU frightened each other over Kiel one afternoon. The two units were then amalgamated and with the improved supply position given an adequate aircraft establishment.

9. The story since then is one of continual development not only of the cameras with the consequent improvement of the photographic quality, but also of the aircraft thus bringing further areas within range. The introduction of the Mosquito early in 1942 was a big step forward in long range reconnaissance, particularly that involving a long sea passage. It also brought with it a great advance in the navigation over the target thanks to the inclusion of an observer.

10. On the interpretation or intelligence side, the development has also been a continuous process since the early days of the 'Battle of Britain'. Obviously with improved photography the scope of the interpreter has increased out of all recognition. It has been an interesting development, tied up very closely with the development of the PR aircraft and the

cameras themselves. Successful photographic reconnaissance is obviously dependant on the experience, first, of those who have to operate the aircraft, and second, those who have to interpret the results. For the interpreter the secret of success lies in his ability to recognize abnormal activity, coupled with regular reconnaissance of focal points so that any change or movement made by the enemy will be reported by him immediately.

Headquarters No. 6 (PR) Group
4th October 1944
(National Archives AIR 25/790)

Appendix VI

Notes on the Work of PR Squadrons

When the war began, photographic reconnaissance as we understand it today was in its infancy. It has now developed into a large organization that covers every theatre of war and daily brings accurate information to the naval, military and air commanders. Side by side with the growth of the PR squadrons themselves, there has been created a band of experts who scan and interpret the photographs as they come in; together these are known as the Photographic Interpretation Unit. Their skill and experience enable them to extract detailed information from photographs which often appear ordinary and uninteresting to the uninitiated.

Sorties by PR squadrons now cover an immense variety of subjects. During the late summer and autumn of 1940, shipping and port activity along the invasion coast were of vital interest. The Channel ports were photographed at least twice a day and a constant watch was thus kept on the accumulation of barges which assembled between Antwerp and Le Havre.

More recently, damage assessment has come to occupy a large proportion of the activities of the squadrons. Reconnaissance of targets and areas attacked by Bomber Command is carried out at the earliest opportunity after a raid. Photographs have often been obtained within a few hours of the departure of the last bomber from the target. After a heavy raid an early reconnaissance does not usually produce photographs that are suitable for real damage assessment owing to the intense smoke from many fires. Even so, the reconnaissance is important for it will still indicate to Bomber Command the part of the target upon which a heavy concentration has taken place.

But there are many other subjects to be covered. For instance, photography of WT stations has been an important duty, particularly during the development of the enemy radio-location system. Many sorties were flown, quite a number of them from a low level using oblique cameras instead of the usual vertical installations.

Airfield activity is also covered at regular intervals to obtain information concerning the enemy Order of Battle, new types of aircraft in use, alterations to runways, new construction and so on. A constant watch is kept on existing and projected AA defences; the majority have been photographed more than once by PR aircraft; it is not usually necessary to fly special sorties to obtain this information as it can usually be included in other work.

Yet another variety of the work is the preparation of target information. Most cities, towns and factory areas in Germany and occupied territory have been photographed for the purpose of making mosaics from which target maps are completed for the use of bomber crews. The heavy bombing of Western Europe is driving the German factories further to the east but the range of the PR aircraft has increased sufficiently to cover this move.

Finally, routine reconnaissance of U-boat construction centres has greatly helped in calculating the speed of production and the number of U-boats that may be expected to come into operation at any particular time.

The present intake of pilots into the PR OTU consists entirely of experienced pilots, generally those with about 1,000 hours' experience or more; special consideration is given to ex-instructors and second-tour pilots, all of whom are volunteers. Before being accepted for training, each pilot is interviewed at the RAF Station at Benson and a recommendation as to his suitability is made. All pilots must have successfully passed a series of decompression chamber tests. These can be carried out at Benson, and the practice at the moment is to attach pilots for decompression tests and, during this attachment, their interviews are arranged.

PR training is carried out at No. 8 OTU, Dyce, Aberdeenshire. The OTU is equipped with Master IIs and various marks of Spitfires and Mosquitos.

Flying training is divided into single engine and twin engine; each is sub-divided into conversion and advance flying flights. At present both courses last for eight weeks, but the single-engine course is to be reduced to six weeks. The sequence of training in the single-engine flights gives some idea of the ground to be covered.

1. Familiarization flight in Spitfire PR IV aircraft.
2. Height climb to 30,000 feet, followed by further climb to between 35,000 and 38,000 feet.
3. Cross-country practice at 30,000 feet.
4. Photography in local area from 30,000 feet.
5. Cross-country practice up to 1,000 miles at 30,000 feet taking photographs of pin-points on the route.
6. Oblique photography from 500 to 3,000 feet.
7. Cloud flying and VHF practice.

Twin-engine training differs from this plan only in detail. Throughout flying training, considerable time is given to cross-country practice, and accurate navigation over very long distances, sometime in poor weather, is an essential part of the training. Particular attention has also to be paid to navigation at high altitudes where winds of over 100 mph may be experienced. R/T and W/T silence has to be maintained after take-off on the cross-country practice until within 100 miles of base on the return, so that conditions similar to flying over hostile territory are experienced. As many descents through cloud and as much cloud flying as possible are practised. In all, the twin-engine course should receive 55 flying hours and the new shorter, single-engine course 44.

On operational sorties, the more heavily-defended areas and the shorter distances are usually covered by Spitfires on which some amazingly high speeds have been recorded, while the really long-range reconnaissances are carried out by Mosquitos. At one time these aircraft sometimes flew right across Europe and landed in North Africa. This distance has been considerably reduced now that friendly bases exist in Southern Italy. Operational height is governed by condensation trails, the heights of which vary, always becoming lower in the winter months. The Spitfires are usually able to climb through the 'trail' layer and reach comparative safety, knowing that an aircraft climbing to intercept must itself pass through the layer and advertise its whereabouts. But the Spitfire pilot has a great deal to tackle single-handed. Many people ask how the pilot of a Spitfire knows when he is over the target and when to switch on the camera, for the aircraft is not fitted with any sort of sighting apparatus, and the pilot may be flying in wind conditions of well over 100 mph. In the early stages of training for high altitude photography, the usual mistake is to undershoot the target, so instructions are given to make a longer run than is thought to be really necessary. The run is made, if possible, directly up and down wind. If the run has to be made across wind, the drift may be as much as 15 or 18 degrees. But, after very little practice, pilots become quite expert and rarely miss a target. If more than one run is required to cover a target, care has to be taken not to lose height during the turns. When concentrating on getting over the target a second time, it is quite easy to lose 1,000 to 1,500 feet, which will obviously vary the scale of the photographs taken. Those who have flown at very high altitudes know how easy it is to lose 1,000 feet and how difficult it is to regain the original altitude again. The Spitfire pilots must all be good pilot/navigators and have confidence in their ability to navigate an aircraft up to 600 miles from friendly territory with the aid of a watch, compass and Dalton computer only. It must not be forgotten that during the whole of the time spent on navigating to the target, and subsequently concentrating on photography, a constant watch must be kept for enemy aircraft attempting interception. The pilots and wireless-navigators of Mosquitos have to be prepared to carry out even longer flights, but in these aircraft drifts can be taken and more instruments carried to help navigation.

Appendix VI

One other advantage of the Mosquito is that in it there are two pairs of eyes to spot hostile aircraft.

Flak is not very troublesome at high altitudes, except over some heavily-defended areas. If flak is experienced, an extra sharp look-out has to be kept, for it is a good guide to any enemy fighters that may be on interception patrol.

Besides the valuable information contained in any photographs that have been obtained on a sortie, up-to-the-minute meteorological information can be given to the Met. Office on the conditions over enemy territory. Very accurate reports are usually given by PR pilots, for they habitually fly in clear weather above all cloud; even very severe frontal conditions can usually be crossed at 30,000 feet. In view of the importance of this Met. Information, special attention is paid to lectures on meteorology at the OTU.

PR pilots are always taught to give as accurate visual reconnaissance reports as possible, but apart from reporting fires after bombing raids, and movements of convoys, visual reports from high altitudes are not usually very reliable.

From the beginning of PR flying, all pilots and navigators are taught to have implicit confidence in the oxygen systems of the aircraft they are flying, as oxygen is definitely their lifeline. Enough oxygen is carried to ensure a supply after the total fuel of the aircraft is used. Continued improvements are being made to PR aircraft, the greatest to date being the cockpit heater. It is hoped that the next great improvement will be the introduction of a pressure cabin. The work of PR is so important that every effort must be made to maintain that technical ascendancy without which the work could hardly go on.

Headquarters No. 106 (PR) Group.
4th October 1944.
(National Archives AIR 25/790)

Appendix VII

RAF Station Benson personnel and others buried in St Helen's Churchyard Extension, Benson

Name	Force	Date of death	Age
Sgt F. Blyskal (of Poland)	RAF	26 Nov 1940	20
P/O J.C. Campbell (of Canada)	RAF	7 Nov 1939	20
Sgt N.W. Cantwell	RAF	20 Sep 1940	21
P/O T.M. Couper	RCAF	13 Apr 1941	20
Sgt D.J. Craven	RAF	11 Jun 1940	25
P/O J.M.R. de Jenko-Sokolowski	PAF	1 Oct 1940	32
Sgt D.D. Dunlop	RAF	4 Jun 1942	19
Sgt M.V. Everitt	RAF	24 Jul 1940	19
P/O A.V. Fisher (of New Zealand)	RAF	6 Aug 1940	23
P/O J.A. Grierson	RNZAF	7 Dec 1941	21
Sgt C.C. Henderson	RAF	20 Sep 1940	23
F/O P.J. Hugo	RAF	8 Jan 1944	21
Sgt J.D. Hunt	RAF	28 Dec 1940	19
P/O A. Ignaszak	PAF	26 Nov 1940	27
Cpl N.G. Jones	RAF	12 Mar 1941	unk
AC1 R.A.W. Keogh	RAF	18 Oct 1939	20
P/O W. Makarewicz	PAF	26 Nov 1940	25
Sgt D. McLean	RCAF	18 Apr 1941	22

Appendix VII

Sgt O. Odstrcilek (of Czechoslovakia)	RAF	30 Sep 1940	29
Sgt H.W. Parry	RAF	19 Jun 1941	19
Sgt C.D. Perry DFM	RAF	14 Jun 1940	29
AC1 J. Phypers	RAF	12 Jun 1943	39
Sgt W. Robb	RAF	29 Jul 1940	18
Flt Lt L.J. Rooney (of South Africa)	RAF	28 Dec 1940	25
F/O M.L.H. Rose	RAF	8 Jan 1944	25
P/O B.P. Thomson (of New Zealand)	RAF	11 Jun 1940	20
P/O F.H.S. West	RAF	28 Feb 1941	23

St Helen's Churchyard Extension in Benson showing headstones of the Commonwealth War Graves Commission and the Polish and Czechoslovakian Forces.

Appendix VIII

RAF Station Benson personnel commemorated on the Runnymede Memorial

[The panel numbers refer to the place within the memorial cloisters where the name can be found. The names of 20,455 men and women with no known graves are recorded here.]

AITKEN, F/Sgt James McGinn, 1552265, RAF (VR),
  541 Squadron. 21 January 1944. Age unknown. Panel 215.

ASKEW, F/O George Douglas, 151269, RAF (VR),
  544 Squadron. 11 August 1944. Age 21. Panel 204.

AYRES, Flt Lt Robert William, DFC, 40292, PRU
  25 May 1941. Age 20. Panel 29.

BARBER, P/O Charles Bertram, 47734, RAF (VR),
  140 Squadron, 24 April 1942. Age 22. Panel 68.
  See diary entry for 24 April 1942.

BLACKWOOD, P/O Francis John, OBE, 46821, 140 Squadron,
  2 June 1942. Age 28. Panel 68.

BLAIR, F/O Colin Campbell, 77781, RAF (VR), PRU,
  1 September 1941. Age 26. Panel 29.

BOWES, P/O Samuel, 44672, PRU,
  30 June 1941. Age 25. Panel 31.

BOYD, W/O Kenneth Leslie, 411381, RNZAF, 540 Squadron,
  21 August 1944. Age 24. Panel 263.

Appendix VIII

BRIGGS, Sgt Leonard, 758051, RAF (VR), PRU,
2 December 1941. Age 21. Panel 40.

BUCKINGHAM, F/Sgt Henry Francis, 1322657, RAF (VR),
542 Squadron, 25 February 1944. Age 22. Panel 40.

BUCKLAND, AC2 James Crompton, 619734, 63 Squadron,
1 December 1939. Age 19. Panel 3.

BUSBRIDGE, P/O George Norcott, 87428, PRU,
10 September 1941. Age 26. Panel 31.

CAMERON, P/O Angus, 41900, 63 Squadron,
1 December 1939. Age 22. Panel 1

CHANDLER, P/O John Derek, 79518, RAF (VR), PRU,
16 February 1941. Age unknown. Panel 31.

CHARLES-JONES, P/O John Kenneth, 44661, PRU,
27 July 1941. Age 23. Panel 31

COVENTRY, P/O Charles Robey, 40606, 63 Squadron,
1 December 1939. Age 27. Panel 1.

CRUIKSHANK, Sgt Bernard Herbert, 637524,
540 Squadron, 3 March 1943. Age 35. Panel 146.

CUMMING, F/O Ernest Robert, J/18599, RCAF, 542 Squadron,
10 April 1944. Age 21. Panel 245.

DAWSON, F/Sgt Dennis Charles, 1580354, RAF (VR),
540 Squadron, 23 August 1944. Age 21. Panel 217.

DENSHAM, Flt Lt Arthur Roy, 41157, PRU,
27 March 1942. Age 29. Panel 65.

EDWARDS, F/O Allen Grayson, 416166, RAAF, 541 Squadron,
25 January 1943. Age 35. Panel 187.

EVANS, F/Sgt Charles Hope, 1379807, RAF (VR),
543 Squadron, 28 February 1943. Age 20. Panel 136.

FUGE, Flt Lt Brian Kenneth Levinge, 41394, 541 Squadron,
19 March 1945. Age 28. Panel 265.

GEORGE, P/O Daniel Ernest, 121564, RAF (VR),
540 Squadron, 3 April 1943. Age unknown. Panel 131.

GIBSON, Sgt Alvin Gordon, 581212, 63 Squadron,
1 December 1939. Age 19. Panel 1.

GORMLAY, AC2 Hugh Oliver Wilson, 543996
63 Squadron, 1 December 1939. Age 21. Panel 3.

GOULDEN, F/Sgt Thomas, 1044413, RAF (VR),
541 Squadron, 28 May 1943. Age 24. Panel 136.

GREENWOOD, F/O George Benjamin Dudley, 118419,
RAF (VR), 543 Squadron, 14 February 1943. Age 26. Panel 124.

HANEY, F/O Robert Shirley, 146288, RAF (VR), 540 Squadron,
26 October 1943. Age unknown. Panel 124.

HARDMAN, F/O Donald Francis Ignatius, 411888, RNZAF,
540 Squadron, 3 March 1943. Age 26. Panel 197.

HARRISON, W/O Walter, 740905, RAF (VR), 1 PRU,
1 August 1942. Age 30. Panel 72.

HORSFALL, Sgt Sidney Edward, 921014, RAF (VR), 1 PRU,
4 December 1941. Age 27. Panel 45.

HOWARTH, F/Sgt David Norman, 1086884, RAF (VR),
544 Squadron, 7 April 1944. Age 21. Panel 219.

HUGHES, P/O Trevor Jones, J/17635, RCAF, 544 Squadron,
15 May 1943. Age 30. Panel 176.

JONES, Flt Lt Hayden Mortimer, 42233, 1 PRU,
30 July 1942. Age 26. Panel 65.

JONES, F/Sgt Mervyn Anthony, 748630, RAF (VR), 1 PRU,
3 April 1942. Age 23. Panel 75.
(RAF Benson records show the date as 2 April 1942.)

JONES, Flt Lt Eric Reginald, 68781 RAF (VR) 544 Squadron,
14 September 1944. Age 30. Panel 202.

Appendix VIII

KING, F/Sgt Herbert Allan, 605474, RAF (VR), 542 Squadron, 14 April 1944. Age 25. Panel 219.

LANE, Sgt Geoffrey George, 1322909, RAF (VR), 540 Squadron, 13 June 1943. Age 22. Panel 156.

LEAVITT, Flt Lt Robert Frederick DFC, 42238, 1 PRU, 21 September 1941. Age 25. Panel 29.

LENTON, Sqn Ldr Reginald Arthur, MC, DFC, 42315, 540 Squadron, 26 October 1943. Age 28. Panel 118.

LOASBY, F/O Laurence David, 36242, 1 PRU, 10 April 1941. Age 23. Panel 30.

LUEPKE, Sgt Robert Theodor, 605412, 543 Squadron, 27 October 1942. Age 26. Panel 88.

MAIR, P/O John Drysdale, DFC, 138437, RAF (VR), 540 Squadron, 3 April 1943. Age unknown. Panel 132.

MacLEAN, F/O Roderick Orr, 409641, RAAF, 541 Squadron, 4 November 1943. Age 26. Panel 188.

MANIFOULD, P/O William Kenneth, 81658, RAF (VR) 1 PRU, 10 April 1941. Age unknown. Panel 33.

McCUAIG, Flt Lt Duncan Kennedy, DFC, 67629, RAF (VR), 541 Squadron, 28 September 1944. Age 24. Panel 202.

MILLER, F/Sgt Albert Andrew, R/62889, RCAF, 1 PRU, 20 May 1942. Age 23. Panel 105.

MILLS, F/Sgt Peter Alan, 741481, RAF (VR), 1 PRU, 10 May 1941. Age 23. Panel 37.

MOSS, W/O Thomas John, 521717, 540 Squadron, 3 May 1943. Age 26. Panel 134.

O'CONNELL, Sgt Peter, 403761, RAAF, 1 PRU, 11 August 1942. Age 20. Panel 113.

PANTON, F/O William, DFC, 43150, 1 PRU, 3 May 1941. Age 27. Panel 30.

PARKES, F/O Cranmer Kenneth, 45326, 140 Squadron,
2 June 1942. Age 22. Panel 67.

PAYNE, W/O William John, 754956, RAF (VR),
541 Squadron, 13 January 1943. Age unknown. Panel 134.

PLATTS, Flt Lt George, DFC, 137655, RAF (VR),
541 Squadron, 9 March 1945. Age unknown. Panel 265.

PUNSHON, P/O Jonathan Killingworth, 42724, 1 PRU,
31 March 1941. Age 19. Panel 34.

READ, F/Sgt Howard Richard, 1395940, RAF (VR),
540 Squadron, 21 August 1944. Age 34. Panel 221.

ROBERTS, F/O Leslie Glyn, J/19302, RCAF, 542 Squadron,
6 January 1945. Age 21. Panel 279.

ROGERS, F/Sgt Charles Matthew Thomas, 912386,
RAF (VR), 1 PRU, 22 April 1942. Age 22. Panel 76.

ROTHWELL, F/O Herbert Jack, 128452, RAF (VR),
543 Squadron, 3 July 1943. Age 28. Panel 129.

SARGENT, F/O John Michael Hewlett, 43553, 1 PRU,
9 December 1941. Age unknown. Panel 30.

SAYCE, F/O Patrick Campbell, 84331, RAF (VR), 1 PRU,
27 July 1942. Age 22. Panel 67.

SCAFE, Flt Lt William John, 43113, 1 PRU,
7 September 1942. Age unknown. Panel 66.

STAPLETON, P/O Harold Arthur, 191707, RAF (VR),
544 Squadron, 12 April 1945. Age 22. Panel 268.

SUCKLING, F/O Michael Frank, 42907, 1 PRU,
21 July 1941. Age 21. Panel 30.

SUTTON, F/O George Nevil, 125815, RAF (VR),
540 Squadron, 3 May 1943. Age 24. Panel 129.

TAFFS, F/O John Clifford, 123031, RAF (VR),
541 Squadron, 7 February 1943. Age 21. Panel 129.

TAYLOR, Sqn Ldr Alistair Lennox, DFC and two bars, 39448,
1 PRU, 4 December 1941. Age 25. Panel 28.

THORNTON, F/Sgt George Thomas, 994179, RAF (VR),
1 PRU, 27 July 1942. Age unknown. Panel 76.

TOMLINSON, F/Sgt Robert Duncan Campbell, 905231,
RAF (VR), 1 PRU, 18 March 1942. Age 30. Panel 76.

TULLY, F/O John Leahy, 404189, RAAF, 1 PRU,
30 July 1942. Age 28. Panel 111.

WALKER, F/O Gavin William, 114418, RAF (VR), 1 PRU,
27 September 1942. Age 24. Panel 67.

WARWICK, Flt Lt Edmund Vernon, 117037, RAF (VR),
544 Squadron, 12 April 1945. Age 23. Panel 266.

WRIGHT, Sgt Arthur George, 1336470, RAF (VR),
540 Squadron, 13 June 1943. Age 21. Panel 170.

The Runnymede Memorial

After the 1939 – 1945 War, it was decided that in the United Kingdom there should be a memorial to airmen who lost their lives while serving from bases in the United Kingdom, Iceland, The Faroe Islands, Northern Ireland and the Azores, and from bases on the Continent of Europe in France, Holland, Belgium, Germany, Denmark, Norway, Finland, Luxembourg, Czechoslovakia and Russia. They served in Bomber, Fighter, Coastal, Transport, Flying Training and Maintenance Commands, and came from all parts of the British Commonwealth and Empire.

In 1949 a site on Cooper's Hill, within the Urban District of Egham and overlooking the valley of the Thames at Runnymede, was offered to the Imperial War Graves Commission, and was gratefully accepted in October 1949; on that site was erected the memorial here described.

The design consists of a cloister planned to record the names of the 20, 455 airmen here commemorated. On the far side of the cloister there is a tower, containing a vaulted room or shrine as a place for contemplation. At the southern side of the site are entrance gates to a central avenue, which leads to a three-arched portico giving access to the cloisters. The cloisters on the edge of the wooded hill overlooking the Thames have curved wings, terminating in two look-outs, one facing towards Windsor and the other towards the London airport at Heath Row. The tower has a central arched opening, above which are three sculptured figures representing Justice, Victory and Courage, and the turret is surmounted by a crown. On the river side of the shrine is a balcony, giving a fine view of the Thames Valley and, on a clear day, of seven counties. Two spiral staircases lead to a gallery from which a further staircase gives access to the roof.

The names of the airmen commemorated here are inscribed on the stone reveals of the narrow windows in the cloister and the look-outs. The light coming through the window slits will illuminate the reveals, giving them something of the appearance of partially opened stone books, on which the names can easily be read.

In the centre of the cloister rests the Stone of Remembrance. Above the three-arched entrance to the cloister is a great stone eagle with the Royal Air Force motto 'Per Ardua Ad Astra'; on each side is the inscription; 'In this cloister are recorded the names of twenty thousand airmen who have no known grave. They died for freedom in raid and sortie over the British Isles and the lands and seas of Northern and Western Europe.' In the beautifully engraved glass of the great window of the shrine two angels hold a scroll on which appear the following verses from Psalm CXXXIX:

> If I climb up into Heaven, Thou art there:
> If I go down to Hell, Thou art there also.
> If I take the wings of the morning, and
> remain in the uttermost parts of the sea;
> Even there also shall Thy hand lead me,
> And Thy right hand shall hold me.

Appendix IX

RAF Station Benson Gate Guard Spitfire EN343

On 1 September 1988 the station commander at RAF Benson, Group Captain Philip G. Pinney, wrote to the author to ask for help in identifying a Spitfire that had had a particular success in the photographic reconnaissance role during the Second World War. He explained that the Air Force Board had taken the decision to replace the genuine gate guardian Spitfire with a life-size replica and was anxious to choose an aircraft that had particular relevance to RAF Benson. He realized that it would be difficult to replicate the majesty of a genuine aircraft, especially as the model Spitfire that was being proposed was a F IX fighter version, but had been assured by the Ministry of Defence that the model could be painted in PR colours.

Following research, it was suggested that the model should be based on a Spitfire that had been converted from a Mark F IX airframe to become a Mark XI and EN343, which had served with 542 Squadron at Benson, was chosen. Not only did it fit the basic physical requirements, having been a conversion, it was also the aircraft used to take the famous wartime photographs of the breached Möhne dam following the raid by 617 Squadron in May 1943.

Armed with this information Group Captain Pinney was able to contact the Ministry of Defence with a list of changes that would be required to make the model look like a PR XI Spitfire and by the end of February 1989 permission had been granted to undertake the conversion. The work was to be carried out by the manufacturers, Feggans Brown Limited of London and the planned changes were as follows:

The cannons, cannon wing stubs and cannon housings were to be removed from the wings.

Two replacement cine gun housings were to be cast and modelled onto the aircraft.

The tail wheel was to be retracted.

Three camera ports were to be cut out and modelled on to the fuselage; two on the underside and the third in the port inspection panel.

The windscreen was to be replaced with a one piece, wrap around polycarbonate windscreen.

The chin cowling in the engine section was to be remodelled.

The converted aircraft parts were delivered to RAF Station Benson at the beginning of June 1989 and were stored in a hangar while the Spitfire was assembled and a plinth built.

On Friday 17 November 1989 at 1500 hours a ceremony was held to unveil the replica EN343. Station Commander, Group Captain Philip Pinney addressed the assembled audience and Squadron Leader F.G. Fray who, as a flying officer, had taken the photos of the Dams, performed the honours. The ceremony was attended by invited guests including Mrs Fray, the author and some members of his family and Flight Lieutenant Gordon Puttick who had been a PR pilot and had been shot down and captured on 13 May 1944. Flight Lieutenant Puttick went on to become the Honorary Secretary of the PR Association and organized many enjoyable reunions at RAF Benson in the years following the end of the war. The ceremony was also attended by local journalists and a camera crew from Central Television.

The commemorative plaque which Squadron Leader Fray unveiled had been placed in front of the Spitfire and read:

> This replica of EN343, the Spitfire PR XI of 542 Squadron which took the first photographs of the Dams Raid, stands to commemorate the officers, airmen and airwomen who served at Royal Air Force Benson from 1939 – 1945, as well as all those who served on the Photographic Reconnaissance Units and Squadrons from this station. In particular we remember those who failed to return.
> **PER ARDUA AD ASTRA**

The real EN343.

Replica EN343 and commemorative plaque.

An illustrated case had been constructed by Corporal Mick Pocknell to stand with the plaque in front of Spitfire EN343 and gave the following additional information:

Spitfire PR IX (EN343)

This replica of Spitfire PR IX (EN343) was placed here in 1989 to commemorate the officers and airmen who served at Royal Air Force Benson from 1939 – 1945, including the personnel who served on the Photographic Reconnaissance Units and Squadrons from this station during World War II. In particular, it commemorates all personnel from RAF Benson who have given their lives in the service of this country.

The replica of EN343 replaces Spitfire PR XIX 'PM651X', which had stood as Gate Guardian at RAF Benson from 1973 until 1989 when it was removed to become the centre piece of the new Photographic Reconnaissance Unit display being constructed at the RAF Museum, Hendon. In doing so PM651X will demonstrate to the widest audience more about the sterling work of Benson's PRU which played such a fundamental part in winning the strategic and tactical battles of World War II.

The original EN343 was built at Chattis Hill as a F IX. It was converted to the PR XI standard before being taken onto the strength of No. 542 Squadron at RAF Benson in February 1943. After its initial acceptance checks it flew its first operational sortie on 4 March 1943 when Flying Officer Efford photographed Bremen; a full list of the operational sorties flown by this aircraft is shown alongside. [See pages 177-9] Perhaps the most famous occurred when, on the morning of 17 May 1943, Flying Officer F.G (Gerry) Fray flew a 7 hours 25 minutes sortie [sic] to photograph the Möhne and Sorpe Dams following the attacks by No. 617 (Dambuster) Squadron the previous night. For this sortie, Flying Officer Fray was awarded the DFC.

Regrettably we have no complete record of the operational sorties flown by EN343 with the Desert Air Force at the end of the North African campaign and during the preparations for the Allied invasions of Sicily and Italy. Subsequently, after EN343 returned to Benson, it was flown by Air Commodore J.N. Boothman AFC, a former Station Commander who had become

AOC No. 106 (PR) Group. Years earlier, he had achieved fame as the winner of the Schneider Trophy in the Spitfire's famous forebear, the Supermarine S6.

In March 1944 Flight Lieutenant Witherick was intercepted by German fighters over Antwerp in EN343 but, even then, was able to use the superior performance of the Spitfire PR XI to evade the enemy. Subsequently in July 1944, the aircraft was deployed to No. 8 (PR) Operational Training Unit at Dyce for training future PR pilots. This unit moved to Haverfordwest in West Wales in January 1945 where, sadly, the original EN343 was written off on 11 March 1946 after suffering an engine failure on take-off.

This replica of EN343 was unveiled at a small ceremony in November 1989 by Squadron leader F.G. Fray who won his DFC on the original EN343. The replica helps reinforce the strong links which have always been maintained between the Station, the Photographic Reconnaissance Unit and all the other former Units and Squadrons who have served at Royal Air Force Benson.

Technical Details

Span 36' 10" Length 30' 0"   Weight 8040 lbs fully laden
Max Speed 417 mph at 24,000 ft
Max Cruise 397 mph at 31,000 ft
Max Ceiling 44,000 ft
Camera fits 2 x F52 vertical (36 ins lens)
or
2 x F20 (8 ins lens) and 1 x F52 (20 ins lens)
or
2 x F28 (8 ins lens) and 1 x F24 (14 ins lens)

Spitfire PR XI 'EN343'
Operational Sorties flown from RAF Benson

Date	Pilot	Target
4 Mar 43	Fg Off F.H. Efford	Bremen
5 Mar 43	Fg Off L. McMillan	Rotterdam & Hamm
7 Mar 43	Fg Off D.G. Scott	Hamm & Essen
7 Mar 43	Flt Lt B.J. Macmaster	Essen
8 Mar 43	Fg Off E.G. Searle	Berlin
15 Mar 43	Fg Off J.H. Shelmerdine	Essen & Liege

17 Mar 43	Fg Off A. G. Paus	Berlin
18 Mar 43	Sgt T.P. Turnbull	Leculot & Blankenburghe
18 Mar 43	Fg Off F.H. Efford	Liege
29 Mar 43	Fg Off J.H. Shelmerdine	Duisberg & Liege
2 Apr 43	Fg Off A. G. Paus	St Nazaire & Lorient
4 Apr 43	Fg Off L. McMillan	St Nazaire & Lorient
4 Apr 43	Fg Off A. G. Paus	Dieppe & Rouen
5 Apr 43	Fg Off F.H. Efford	Trier
16 Apr 43	Fg Off J.H. Shelmerdine	Stuttgart
16 Apr 43	Fg Off D.G. Scott	Stuttgart
18 Apr 43	Sgt V.B. White	Mannheim
18 Apr 43	Fg Off D.G. Scott	Romilly
20 Apr 43	Sgt T. Goulden	Boulogne
7 May 43	Fg Off E.G. Searle	Duisberg & Essen
12 May 43	Fg Off J.H. Shelmerdine	Duisberg & Essen
14 May 43	Fg Off D.G. Scott	Kiel
15 May 43	Fg Off F.H. Efford	Bochum
16 May 43	Sgt T. Goulden	Heligoland & Kiel
17 May 43	Fg Off F.G. Fray	The Dams
28 May 43	Sgt P.J. Spencer	Rotterdam & The Hook
28 May 43	Fg Off D.G. Scott	Rotterdam & The Hook
5 Jun 43	Sgt V.B. White	Strasbourg

EN343 was deployed to North Africa in June 1943 for the collection of Reconnaissance information by the Desert Air Force in the preparation for an execution of the Allied landings in Sicily and Italy. Regrettably we do not have a record of the sorties flown, due to the rapidly changing situation in the theatre at that time. After EN343 was returned to RAF Benson in December 1943, it flew the following operational sorties with 542 Squadron:

APPENDIX IX

Date	Pilot	Target
4 Dec 43	Flt Lt R.W. Witherick	Dunkirk & Calais
4 Dec 43	FS V.B. White	Paris & Targets en route
20 Dec 43	Fg Off A.R. Graham	Cherbourg
22 Dec 43	Air Cdre J.N. Boothman	Pas de Calais
23 Dec 43	Fg Off E.G. Searle	Abbeville
24 Dec 43	Fg Off A.R. Graham	Cherbourg
28 Dec 43	FS V.B. White	Pas de Calais
30 Dec 43	Fg Off D.G. Scott	Pas de Calais
31 Dec 43	Fg Off T.P. Turnbull	Abbeville
5 Jan 44	Fg Off D.G. Scott	Kassel & Liege
11 Jan 44	Fg Off B.R. Kenwright	Berlin
21 Jan 44	Flt Lt R.W. Witherick	Zeebrugge
25 Jan 44	FS H. Bridle	Soesterburg
4 Feb 44	Fg Off J.H. Dixon	Le Havre & Abbeville
6 Feb 44	Fg Off D.G. Scott	Pas de Calais
14 Feb 44	Fg Off A.R. Graham	Pas de Calais
22 Feb 44	Flt Lt R.W. Witherick	Dieppe
24 Feb 44	Plt Off V.B. White	Stuttgart
25 Feb 44	FS J.A Deighton	Le Crotary & Beauvais
5 Mar 44	Fg Off L. McMillan	Salzwedal & Lübeck
8 Mar 44	Flt Lt R.W. Witherick	Rotterdam & Antwerp
25 Mar 44	FS J.A Deighton	Brussels
27 Mar 44	FS H. Bridle	Essen & Duisberg
30 Mar 44	Plt Off V.B. White	Job 910
8 May 44	Plt Off L.G. Roberts	Antwerp
10 May 44	Plt Off L.G. Roberts	Le Havre
12 May 44	Plt Off V.B. White	Siegfried Line
20 May 44	FS L.B. Baker	Bayeaux Area

Group Captain P. G. Pinney LVO ADC RAF
and Squadron Leader F. G. Fray DFC.

L to R: Author's wife, author, Squadron Leader F. G. Fray
and Flight Lieutenant G. W. Puttick DFC.

'After a very early call I struggled into the air at 0730 hours. Trails at 30,500 and weather cloudless. Crossed in Ijmuiden and when 150 miles away from target saw floods stretching towards Ruhr. Did several runs when saw two hostiles approaching from NE. Beat it for base and landed 1105 with the news and amidst a vast concourse of people.'

Flying Officer F.G. Fray
'B' Flight 542 Squadron
17 May 1943

Sources

Whilst the majority of the information in the diary has been taken from RAF Operations Record Books, some facts have been provided by individuals, other records at the National Archives and the Commonwealth War Graves Commission. Aircraft marks and serial numbers were checked against the records in *British Military Aircraft Serials 1911-1971* by Bruce Robertson, Pub: Ian Allan, 1971 and *Spitfire – The History* by Eric B. Morgan and Edward Shacklady, Pub: Key Publishing Ltd, 1987. Some of these records have conflicting information.

The personal information on page 8 about Polish airmen Franciszek Blyskal, Antoni Ignaszak and Wladyslaw Makarewicz, and that about Marian de Jenko-Sokolowski on page 8 was obtained as a result of correspondence with Jos van Alphen. The information about Marek Ostoja-Slonski and his family on pages 99-100 was from Mr van Alphen's website www.polishwargraves.nl

Information about Czechoslovak pilot, Otakar Odstrcilek, on page 8 was provided by Pavel Vancata of Prague, Czech Republic. http://cz-raf.hyperlink.cz

The details on page 100 of the two German airmen who were killed when their aircraft crashed at Andridge Farm were provided by Karin Bassti of the *Volksbund Deutsche Kriegsgräberfürsorge* [German War Graves Commission] after the Revd Andrew Hawken of St Helen's Church, Benson, confirmed that their remains had been exhumed and moved elsewhere.

Many thanks to all concerned.

Index

Page numbers in italics denote illustrations

Aachen, 125
Abbeville, 104
Abingdon, 86
Acott, Flying Officer later Squadron
  Leader W.R., 81, *82*, 84
Adcock, Flight Lieutenant D., 120
Adlam, Flying Officer F.P., 131, 132
Afrikanda, 50
Aircraft
  Airspeed
    Horsa
      HG755, 102

  Avro
  Anson
    AX180, 30
    AX228, 30, 55
    AX229, 30, 37
    DJ182, 38, 55
    N5073, 3
    N9908, 25
    W2635, 30, 55
    W2637, 30, 55

  Avro
  Lancaster
    N6263, 131
    ND989, 106, 107
    RF150, 134

  Bristol
  Blenheim
    K7143, 12
    R6080, 32
    T2444, 15
    V5736, 14
    V5808, 12
    Z5806, 32
    Z5807, 32

  Fairey
  Battle
    K9393, 6
    K9397, 2
    K9403, 6
    K9406, 6
    K9416, 8
    K9460, 6
    L5071, 8
    L5079, 7
    P2271, 6
    P2274, 2

  Curtiss
  P-40 Tomahawk
    2596M, 23

  de Havilland
  Mosquito
    DD615, 53
    DD659, 53
    DK284, 53
    DK310, 49
    DK311, 53
    DK314, 53
    DK315, 53, 71
    DK320, 53, 143
    DZ517, 85
    DZ523, 77
    DZ532, 77
    LR405, 87
    LR406, 107, 123
    LR407, 98
    LR408, 107
    LR412, 86, 99
    LR416, 104
    LR419, 90
    LR420, 88
    LR421, 107
    LR424, 103

LR426, 130
LR430, 98
LR431, 115
LR433, 118
LR434, 108
LR435, 120
LR436, 88
LR478, 89
MM231, 124
MM232, 96
MM239, 103
MM240, 118
MM245, 120
MM247, 103
MM273, 115
MM276, 136
MM300, 122
MM328, 134
MM351, 125
MM352, 112
MM354, 121
MM355, 121
MM360, 121
MM365, 113
MP469, 27
NS396, 133
NS500, 134
NS504, 118
NS505, 113
NS633, 123
NS637, 131
NS654, 125
NS791, 127
NS814, 133
RF971, 133
W4050, 27
W4051, 20, 23, 27, 53, 60, 61, 75
W4054, 27, 53, 72, 76
W4055, 27, 33
W4056, 38
W4058, 51, 53
W4059, 29, 53
W4060, 67, 68
W4061, 53
W4062, 35, 36
W4063, 35, 36
W4067, 46
W4089, 45

de Havilland
 Tiger Moth
  N9305, 55
  R4958, 81

Douglas
 DC-3 Dakota
  FL597, 103

Handley Page
 Halifax
  JB856, 84
  LK794, 115
  LW128, 112
  LW579, 103
  NP681, 123

Martin
 Maryland
  AR730, 17
  AR734, 17
  AR744, 44, 55

Miles
 Master
  W8786, 45

North American
 P-51 Mustang
  FB182, 131
  FD504, 89

Short
 Stirling
  EF497, 87

Supermarine
 Spitfire
  AA781, 48
  AA783, 32, 37
  AA784, 54
  AA787, 37
  AA790, 54
  AA793, 54
  AA795, 42
  AA797, 39
  AA798, 39
  AA800, 46
  AA801, 30, 32
  AA802, 50
  AA803, 55
  AA806, 54, 58, 60
  AA807, 53, 76
  AA808, 53, 69
  AA809, 54, 65
  AA810, 37
  AA813, 35
  AA814, 48
  AB118, 54, 58
  AB119, 41
  AB120, 48
  AB121, 54
  AB123, 54

INDEX

AB124, 54, 143
AB125, 65
AB127, 43
AB128, 54, 69
AB129, 43
AB130, 49
AB132, 54
AB300, 37
AB301, 46
AB302, 53
AB303, 54
AB305, 54
AB306, 55
AB307, 39
AB309, 53, 60
AB311, 54
AB314, 48
AB317, 49
AB422, 49
AB424, 55
AB425, 41
AB427, 55
AB428, 63, 69
AB430, 54, 64
AD121, 58
AR234, 44
AR235, 55
AR242, 54, 143
AR245, 38
AR257, 54, 69
AR260, 54
AR261, 54
BP881, 54, 64
BP884, 54
BP886, 54
BP887, 48
BP889, 55
BP891, 53
BP907, 41
BP917, 55
BP918, 54
BP919, 54
BP921, 45
BP922, 45, 54
BP923, 54
BP924, 49
BP926, 54, 142
BP929, 72
BP937, 53
BR412, 86
BR415, 75
BR417, 46, 68
BR420, 55
BR650, 54

BR658, 54
BR660, 53, 64
BR661, 53
BR666, 55, 62
BR669, 62
BS490, 81
BS501, 71
BS502, 102
EN149, 75
EN151, 68
EN154, 89, *95*
EN330, 104
EN342, 71
EN343, 78, 173-8
EN348, 74
EN385, 64
EN411, 80
EN417, 89
EN424, 104
EN503, 98
EN668, 105
EN669, 94
EN682, 118
EN685, 107
K9787, 20
MB782, 81
MB788, 112
MB789, 90
MB790, 81
MB792, 83
MB902, 105, 112
MB908, 89
MD197, 128
N3111, 20, 55
N3117, 15, 33
N3241, 14
P9385, 12
P9550, 9
P9552, 15
P9561, 11
P9565, 54
PA855, 100
PA945, 124
PC857, 131
PL882, 126
PL887, 126
PL889, 128
PL904, 124
PL906, 126
PL919, 127
PM148, 130
PR777, 104
PS831, 133
R6610, 32

R6805, 15
R6902, 22
R6903, 22
R6964, 62
R7028, 41
R7033, 29
R7035, 38
R7036, 41
R7037, 26, 44
R7038, 51
R7039, 25
R7040, 33
R7041, 63
R7042, 53, 68
R7043, 29
R7044, 64
R7056, 39
R7070, 17
R7139, 55
R7142, 33
R7147, 30
R7211, 54
RM627, 130
RM631, 130
RM632, 128
RM633, 113
RM635, 131
X4333, 26, 140
X4335, 17
X4383, 22
X4384, 12, 26
X4385, 22, 26
X4491, 23, 25
X4492, 41
X4493, 22, 23
X4494, 22
X4495, 15
X4496, 17
X4497, 23
X4498, 22, 140
X4500, 25
X4501, 23, 140
X4502, 44
X4672, 30, 32, 54
X4786, 26, 55
X4907, 38

Vickers
Wellington
L4342, 13
LN614, 102
R1285, 12
Z1417, 44, 55, 58
Z1418, 44, 55, 58

Aitken, Flight Sergeant J., 98
Alden, Mr F.G., 124
Alderney, 44
Allen, Pilot Officer B.K., 38-9
Allonby, LAC A., 105
Alten Fjord, 114
Amiens, 42
Anderson, Pilot Officer A.B., 63
Anderson, Pilot Officer J.R., 1-2
Anderson, Squadron Leader W.B., 112
Andrew, Sergeant J.F., 123
Arbroath, 85
Arkle, Sergeant J., 80
Arnold, Flight Lieutenant K.F., 22
Arnsberg, 131
Ashton, Corporal, 50
Ashton, LAC, 50
Askew, Flying Officer G.D., 120
Aston Rowant, 69
Aston, Squadron Leader B.G., 98
Atkinson, Flight Lieutenant R.W., 120
Ayer, Flying Officer J.B., 39
Ayres, Flying Officer R.W., 17

Baird, Flying Officer S.I., 86
Ball, Flying Officer later Squadron Leader A.H.W., 29, 96
Ball, Warrant Officer M.H., 41
Barber, Flying Officer A.P.L., 35
Barber, Pilot Officer C.B., 42
Bardney, 142
Barents, Pilot Officer R.J., 120, 122
Barfleur, 37
Barraclough, Pilot Officer, 51
Barratt, Air Marshal Sir Arthur S., 45, 46
Bartley, Flight Sergeant M.L., 96
Barwell, Pilot Officer G.F., 2
Beamish St John, Group Captain C.E., 105, 145
Beck, Flying Officer J.C., 103
Bedford, LAC T., 74
Beer, Corporal, 50
Belfast, 141
Ben, Wing Commander R.C. van der, 84
Benton, Flying Officer J.H., 85
Berck-sur-Mer, 33
Beresford, Squadron Leader, 10
Bergen, 33, 38, 46, 68, 85
Berlin, 90, 109
Bexhill, 9
Bielefeld, 130

Index

Bingen, 49
Bisham, 115
Bishops Stortford, 29
Bismarck, 17
Blackpool, 13
Blackwood, Pilot Officer F.J., *40*, 41-2, 44
Blair, Flying Officer C.C., *24*, 25
Bloomfield, Flying Officer G.J., 125
Blyskal, LAC F., 8-9
Blyth, Pilot Officer R.L.C., 44
Bohlenlutzendorf, 130
Böhlitz-Ehrenberg, 100
Bone, 62
Bonnar, Flying Officer N.J., *150*
Boothman, Air Commodore J.N., 80, 84, 86, 88, 145
Bordeaux, 43, 69, 84, 89, 94
Borowski, *Grefreiter* Karl-Heinz, 100
Boscastle, 3
Boscombe Down, 86, 133
Boulogne, 89
Bourne, Pilot Officer I.D., 42
Bowes, Pilot Officer S., 20
Bowhill, Sir Frederick W., 10
Boyd, Pilot Officer E.G.G., 107
Boyd, Warrant Officer K.L., 121
Braathen, Pilot, 143
Bradwell Bay, 126
Brandenburg, 108-9
Braun, Flying Officer E.C., 100
Bremen, 41, 48, 50, 51, 124
Bremerhaven, 41, 48, 49
Brennan, Flight Lieutenant C.A., 62
Breslau, 77, 122
Brest, 13, 17, 23, 25, 33
Brew, Flying Officer J.R., 75
Briggs, Sergeant L., 33
Britain, ASO Delia, *116*
Bromet, Air Vice Marshal G.R., 10
Brooks, Flying Officer W.G., 130
Brunswick, 115
Brux, 72
Buckingham, Flight Sergeant H.F., 102
Buckland, AC2 J.C., 3
Bude, 3
Bullimore, Flight Sergeant P., 122
Busbridge, Pilot Officer G.N., 25
Bussey, Group Captain J., 23, 145

Caen, 32
Cambrai, 15
Cameron, Pilot Officer A., 3
Campbell, Sergeant A., 75, 80
Campbell, Flying Officer J.R., 112
Campbell, Warrant Officer K.G., 89
Cannock Chase, 100
Cantillion, Pilot Officer A.J.E.G., 48
Capel, Air Commodore A.J., 6
Casablanca, 62
Catterick, 20
Celle, 130
Chadwick, Sergeant, 19
Chalmers, ASO, *117*
Chambers, Flight Sergeant L., 108-10, 122
Chandler, Pilot Officer J.D., 11
Charles-Jones, Pilot Officer J.K., 22-3
Checkendon, 2, 8
Cherbourg, 37, 41, 44, 60, 69, 90
Chipping Warden, 20
Chivenor, 10
Cholsey, 102
Christie, Flying Officer C.A.P., 33-4
Church Fenton, 76
Claert, Pilot Officer L.J.E., 60
Clark, Flying Officer H., 122
Clark, Flight Lieutenant L., 14
Clark, Flying Officer N.R.M., 112
Clarke, Squadron Leader R.F., 29, 30
Clegg, Flight Lieutenant B., 80
Cochrane, LAC, 50
Coddington, Flight Lieutenant H.G.J., 143
Cognac, 94
Cologne, 64, 84, 126
Colquhoun, Group Captain J.W., 140
Coltishall, 108
Cooper, Flying Officer A.E., 124
Cooper, Pilot Officer I.B., 17
Copenhagen, 29
Coquet Island, 143
Corfe Castle, 33
Corunna, 81
Couper, Pilot Officer T.M., 13
Coventry, Pilot Officer C.R., 3
Cowleaze Wood, 103
Craig, Flight Lieutenant, *92*
Crakanthorp, Flying Officer later Flight Lieutenant G.R., 56, 69, 126
Crow, Flying Officer later Flight Lieutenant A.M., 89, 127
Croy, Flying Officer D., 65, *66*
Cruikshank, Sergeant B., 71
Cumming, Pilot Officer E.R., 104
Cussons, Flying Officer R., 56

Custance, Flight Sergeant M.M.U., 72
Cuthbertson, Sergeant A., 84
Cuxhaven, 49

Dagworthy, Sergeant, *92*
Danzig, 120, 123
Darlington, 141
Davidson, Mac, *66*
Davis, Flight Sergeant J.A., 142
Dawson, Flight Sergeant D.C., 121-2
de Jenko-Sokolowski, Pilot Officer J.M.R., 8
de la Forte, Air Chief Marshal Sir Philip Joubert, 22
Dedelsdorf, 130
Delmenhorst, 46
Den Helder, 121
Densham, Flight Lieutenant A.R., 38, *40*
Depree, Sergeant A.B., 81
Desvies, 62
Devereux, Pilot Officer, 49
Devizes, 112
Dew, Mr A.R., 124
Dickson, Flight Sergeant C., 143
Dieppe, 37, 104
Dodd, Flight Lieutenant later Squadron Leader F.L., 113-15, 131
Dolgelly, 99
Donaghue, Pilot Officer later Flight Lieutenant W.R., 62, 105
Donaldson, Flying Officer R.W., 69
Dornie, 140
Dortmund Ems Canal, 81
Douglas-Hamilton, Squadron Leader Lord David, 118
Douglas-Hamilton, Wing Commander The Lord M.A., 76, 102, 138, 140
Downie, Flying Officer J.A., 112
Dowse, Flying Officer S.H., 15, *16*, 23, 25
Drayton St Leonards, 7
Dresden, 122
Drever, Sergeant F.I., 108
Drew, Flying Officer C.C., 104
Dunkirk, 37
Dunn, Group Captain W.H., 6, 145
Dunsfold, 118
Durbridge, Flying Officer, 128
Durston, Flight Lieutenant E.J., 37
Düsseldorf, 64, 126
Duxbury, Flight Sergeant F.R., 71
Duxford, 45

East Grinstead, 49, 131
Edwards, Pilot Officer A.G., 63, 64
Edzell, 140
Emden, 37, 41, 48
Essen, 71, 81
Etherington, Sergeant, *66*
Evans, Sergeant C.H., 69
Evans, Sergeant F.C., 49
Evans, Sergeant F.J., 65
Evans, Flight Sergeant H.W., 77-8
Ewelme, 88

Fairhurst, Flight Lieutenant, 50
Fairoaks aerodrome, 60
Falun, 110
Farlow, Flying Officer P.N., 107
Fassberg, 130
Featherstone, Sergeant E., 12
Fergusson, Flying Officer W.M., 85
Fermo, 115
Fielden, Flying Officer J., 103, 124
Fielden, Sergeant, 49
Fielding, Flight Lieutenant P.S.A., 98
Fiscalini, Pilot Officer R.J.F., 141
Fleming, Squadron Leader J.G., 122
Flushing, 65
Flux, Flying Officer, *92*
Flynn, Pilot Officer J.K., 14
Ford, 46, 89
Fôret de Nieppe, 120
Fort William, 141
Fortt, Flying Officer E.W.R., 39
Foster, Air Vice-Marshal W.F. MacN., 8
Fraserburgh, 138
Fray, Flying Officer later Squadron Leader F.G. 'Jerry', 78, 79, 174, *180, 181*
Friedrichshafen, 103
Frisian Islands, 108
Fry, Sergeant E.F., 12
Fuge, Flight Lieutenant B.K., 131
Fuller, Corporal, *92*
Furniss, Flying Officer, 50

Gardner, Sergeant A.W., 141
Gatehouse, Flying Officer P.E., 118
Gdynia, 120, 123
Geldern, 112
Genoa, 14, 60
George, Pilot Officer D.E., 74
George, Flying Officer, 142
German aircraft
   Focke-Wulf
      FW190, 81

INDEX 189

Junkers
 Ju88, 7, 11, 109-10
Messerschmitt
 Me109, 15
 Me210, 109
 Me262, 115
Ghent, 64
Gheude, Flight Lieutenant S.L.E.G., 94
Gibraltar, 19, 20, 35, 77, 81
Gibson, Sergeant A.G., 3-4
Gimson, Flying Officer P.G.C., 39
Gleiwitz, 123
Godden, Lieutenant G.F. 131
Goldie, Sergeant J.D., 64
Goodwood, 38
Gormlay, AC2 H.O.W., 3-4
Gorrill, Sergeant V.I., 81, *82*
Gothenburg, 17
Goudy, Sergeant C.M., 84
Gough, AC1 L.F, 144
Goulden, Sergeant T., 80
Grandcamp, 32
Gravenstede, Flight Sergeant D., 89
Greenhill, Flying Officer C.A.S., 23, *24*, 25
Greenwood, Flying Officer G.B.D., 65
Greenwood, Sergeant, 50
Griffiths, Flying Officer W.S., 126
Groningen, 41
Grubb, Pilot Officer A., 73
Gunn, Pilot Officer A., *36*, 37

Hall, Pilot Officer W.C., 14
Hamburg, 26, 46, 48, 80, 94, 124, 128
Hamer, Pilot Officer E.R., 30
Hampson, Flight Lieutenant W., 115
Haney, Pilot Officer R.S., 88
Hanover, 107, 124, 127, 131
Harding, Flying Officer P., 23, *24*
Hardman, Flying Officer D.F.I., 71
Hardman, Sergeant, 50, 51
Harris St John, Pilot Officer C.D., 45, *47*, *66*
Harris, Flying Officer E.J., 49-50
Harrison, Warrant Officer W., 48
Harvey, Sergeant, 139
Hatfield, 20, 23
Hayes, Sergeant J.D., 51, 53
Hays, Flying Officer R.M., 133
Heijden, Squadron Leader P.R.M. van der , 64-5, *67*
Henderson, Flight Sergeant J.W.S., 88-9

Henley, 90, 102
Hennesy, Flying Officer, *92*
Henry, Sergeant V.E.M., 41
Herbert, Flying Officer P.W., 35
Herford, 125
Heston, 9
Higson, Flying Officer D., 51
Hill, Squadron Leader A.E., 56, *57*, 58
Hill, Flight Sergeant E., 113-15
Hill, Pilot Officer L., 131
Hitzacker, 122, 124
HM King George VI, 7, 29
HM Queen Elizabeth, 29
Hodnett, Sergeant L.O., 19
Holland, Flying Officer K.R., 86, 125
Hood, Flight Lieutenant M.D., 56, *57*
Hope, Flight Sergeant S.F., 62
Hornby, Flight Lieutenant, *92*
Hornsey, Sergeant G.E.R., 142
Horsfall, Sergeant S.E., 33
Horten, 74
Howarth, Flight Sergeant D.N, 103
HRH Group Captain the Duke of Kent, 13, *16*
Hughes, Flying Officer later Squadron Leader G.E., 58, 76, *150*
Hughes, Flight Sergeant T.J., 78
Hugo, Flying Officer P.J., 72, 98
Hunter, Flight Sergeant, *73*
Hunter, Pilot Officer later Flying Officer G.C.D., 75, 103, 124
Hustedt, 130
Hutcheson, Pilot Officer I., 38

Ignaszak, Flying Officer A., 8
Ingolstadt, 45
Ipsden, 87
Ipswich, 15
Irving, Pilot Officer J., 107-8
Irwin, Flying Officer J.H., 107

Jenkins, Flight Lieutenant T.R., 121
Jewell, Sergeant F.D., 108
Johnson, Flight Lieutenant R.P., 94
Johnson, Sergeant W., 76, 81
Jolly, Sergeant W.A., 140
Jones, Flight Lieutenant E.R., 123
Jones, Flight Lieutenant H.M., 46
Jones, Flight Sergeant M.A., 39
Jones, Corporal N.G., 13
Jones, Professor R.V., 29
Jones, Sergeant, 29
Jupp, Pilot Officer P.A., 139
Jütebog, 122

Kaa Fjord, 113-14
Kaiser Fahrt Canal, 134
Karno, 64
Kassel, 49
Katwijk, 37
Kelley, Flight Sergeant S.S., 103
Kelly, Warrant Officer J.L., 143-4
Kennedy, Pilot Officer W., 108-10
Kent, Flight Sergeant A.J., 68, 71-2
Keogh, AC1 Class R.A.W., 1-2
Kershaw, Flight Sergeant R.H., 118
Kiel, 23, 29, 48, 49, 83
King, Flight Sergeant H.A., 104
Kingham, Flying Officer R.J., 118
Kingston Bagpuize, 104
Kirwan, Flying Officer E.F., 85
Kohlenbissen, 130
Königsberg, 123
Kristiansand, 46, 63, 74, 85
Kvasse Fjord, 63

La Pallice, 22, 33
Lake Geneva, 83
Lane, Flight Lieutenant, 45
Lane, Sergeant G.G., 81
Larache, 104
Larson, Pilot Officer, 46
Laurencekirk, 142
Lavender, Sergeant J., 67, 69, 71
Lawrence, Sergeant R.M., 69, *70*, 83
Laws, ASO, *117*
Le Creusot, 58
Le Havre, 20, 38, 44, 60, 104
Le Mans, 98
Le Mesurier, Wing Commander E.C., 43, *47*, 144
Le Touquet, 38
Leatham, Flight Lieutenant E., 44
Leather, Group Captain R.T., 145
Leavitt, Flying Officer R.F., 29-30
Lebach, 49
Lee, Flight Lieutenant later Acting Squadron Leader E.D.L., 56, 113
Lee, Sergeant F., 72
Legon, Pilot Officer later Flying Officer F.V., 86, 103-4
Leighton Buzzard, 69
Leipzig, 90, 115, 123
Leith Hill, 88
Lenton, Acting Squadron Leader R.A., 88
Licquorish, Flying Officer D.W., 85-6
Liegnitz, 122
Limat, 44

Linz, 68
Lister, 63
Lizard, 84
Loasby, Flying Officer L, 13-14
Lobban, Flying Officer A.S., 115, 133
Lockyer, Sergeant A.D., 68
Lockyer, Acting Flight Lieutenant F.M., 11
Loder, Flight Lieutenant J.H., 78
Lofts, Flight Lieutenant, 26
Lorient, 26, 65
Lübeck, 46, 80, 124
Lucarotti, Pilot Officer E.F., 49, *52*
Ludham, 81
Luepke, Sergeant R.T., 60
Lukhmanoff, Flight Sergeant G.B., 45
Lumsden, Flight Lieutenant M.S., 125
Lüneburg, 131
Lynham, Wing Commander V.H.P., 78
Lyon, Sergeant E., 143
Lyons, 118

Macdonald, Pilot Officer A., 37
Mackay, Group Captain C.W., 1, 145
Mackay, Flight Lieutenant S.M., 133
MacLean, Flying Officer R.O., 89
Macmerry, 142
Magdeburg, 122
Mair, Pilot Officer J.D., 74
Makarewicz, Flying Officer W., 8
Malcolm, Flying Officer F.I., 43
Mallett, AC2 A.W.R., 11
Manifould, Flying Officer W., 13
Mann, Flying Officer G.E., 85-6
Manston, 75
Marienburg, 123
Marrakech, 62
Martyn, Sergeant F.T., 139
Matthewman, Flight Lieutenant D.L., 118, 120
McCrohan, Sergeant J.J., 68
McCuaig, Flight Lieutenant D., 124
McDonell, Pilot Officer J.D.M., 141
McGinn, Sergeant W.L., 139
McKay, Pilot Officer F.W., 62
McKenzie, Sergeant D.A., 11
McLean, Sergeant D., 13
McMaster, Flying Officer later Flight Lieutenant B.J., *73*, 74
McPherson, Sergeant J.C., 44
Meech, Flight Sergeant J.F., 124
Melun, 49

Index

Merifield, Squadron Leader J.R.H., 102
Metcalf, Flying Officer R.G., 125
Miles, Flight Lieutenant J.S.D., 10
Miles, Sergeant P.J., 140
Miller, Sergeant A.A., 43
Miller, Sergeant H.J., 139
Mills, Sergeant, 9
Mills, Sergeant P.A., 15
Minden, 125
Mitchell, Sergeant K.T., 19
Modane, 89
Montrose, 139
Moody, Flying Officer L., 107
Mooney, Sergeant F.V., 140
Morgan, Sergeant W., 14
Morrell, Flight Sergeant W.R., 123
Mortimer, Pilot Officer, 60
Mosley, Sergeant J.E., 142
Moss, Warrant Officer T.J., 77
Mossley, Flight Sergeant M.A., 121
Moylan, Flying Officer H.P., 123
Mulben, 113
Müller, *Leutnant* Felix, 100
Munich, 107, 118, 126
Murray, Group Captain W.B., 145
Musberg, 130, 131
Muspratt, Flying Officer, 41
Myles, Sergeant, 58

Nantes, 26
Neksø, 134
Nelson, Flying Officer W., 72, 76
Nettlebed, 80
Neustadt, 131
Nevers, 60
Newbury, 80
Newby, Pilot Officer G.N.E., 115
Newcastle, 139
Nichol, Flight Sergeant K.J.H., 128
Nicholson, Flying Officer T., 38
North Weald, 98
Northlew, 63
Nuremburg, 68

O'Connell, Sergeant P., 48
O'Neil, Flight Sergeant D., 68
Oberhausen, 81
Odstrcilek, Warrant Officer O., 7-8
Old Sarum, 32
Oldfield, Flying Officer, *92*
Olsen, Flight Lieutenant O.P., 127
Oporto, 77
Oranienburg, 131
Oslo, 46, 51, 74

Osnabrück, 115
Ostend, 11
Ostoja-Slonski, Flying Officer M., 99-100
Osvetim, 8

Paderborn, 107, 125
Paget, General Sir Bernard C.T., 46, 47
Palmer, Sergeant, 19
Panton, Flying Officer W., 15, *16*
Parchim, 124
Paris, 45, 118, 121
Parkes, Flying Officer C.K., 44
Parkinson, Sergeant J.G., 75, 84
Parrott, Flight Sergeant, 26
Parry, Flight Sergeant D.A.E., 123
Parry, Sergeant H.W., 19
Pas de Calais, 42, 90, 98, 102
Pasewalk, 134
Payne, ACW, *92*
Payne, Warrant Officer W.J., 64
Payne, Flying Officer W.L., 68, 71
Peek, Flight Sergeant E.P.H., 87
Peel, Flying Officer N.R., 32
Perleberg, 131
Perman, Flight Sergeant D.B., 96
Peters, Flying Officer, 19
Phillippeville, 62
Phypers, AC1 J., 80-1
Pike, Flight Sergeant, 60
Pike, Geoffrey, 125
Pilcher, Flight Lieutenant A.S., 90
Pilsen, 77
Pinney, Group Captain Philip G., 173, 174, *180*
Platts, Flight Lieutenant G., 130
Pollard, Flying Officer D., 128
Pontoise, 49
Portal, Air Chief Marshal Sir Charles, 29
Portreath, 77, 81
Power, Sergeant J.P., 68
Preston Crowmarsh, 107
Prinz Eugen, 17, *18*
Punshon, Pilot Officer J.K., 13
Puttick, Flying Officer later Flight Lieutenant G.W., 100, *106*, 107, 174, *180*
Puysseleyr, Flight Lieutenant J.F.V., 128

Quirt, Flying Officer D.F., 85

Ray, Flying Officer, 94
Read, Flight Sergeant H.R., 121

Reid, Flying Officer W., 113
Reinsehlen, 131
Renshaw, Sergeant, 138
Reynolds, Flight Sergeant A.L., 86
Rich, Sergeant G.A., 77
Richards, Flight Lieutenant J.L.H.,
    120, 122, 134
Richardson, Sergeant F.J., 140
Riches, Acting Flight Lieutenant P.,
    99
Ricketts, Flight Lieutenant V.A., 45
Riley, Flight Lieutenant F., 62
Ring, Squadron Leader later Wing
    Commander S.L., 42, 75, 84, 86, 88
Rittman, Flight Sergeant H.M., 104
Robbins, Flying Officer, 1
Roberts, Flying Officer L.G., 128
Roberts, Group Captain B.J.R., 145
Robertson, Flight Lieutenant, 92
Robins, Flying Officer D.F., 90
Robinson, Flight Lieutenant F.A., 56
Robinson, Flying Officer W.E., 134
Robson, Squadron Leader D.A.H.,
    20
Robson, Flight Lieutenant J., 132
Rogers, Flight Sergeant C.M.T., 41
Rohnes, Lieutenant N., 143
Rønne, 134
Roosevelt, Lieutenant Colonel
    Elliott, 51
Roosevelt, President Franklin D., 51
Rose, Pilot Officer later Flying
    Officer M.L.H., 72, 98
Rose, Sergeant P.G., 15
Rositz, 130
Ross, Flight Sergeant V.G, 112-13
Rothwell, Flying Officer H.J., 84
Rotterdam, 13, 39, 65
Rowbotham, Flying Officer J., 126
Ruhland, 122
Ruhr, 15, 105, 113, 128
Rutherford, Flight Lieutenant D.,
    124

Saffery, Squadron Leader J.H., 113
Salwey, Squadron Leader D., *79*, 80
San Severo, 103
Sandown, 42
Sargent, Flying Officer J.M.H., 33
Sayce, Flying Officer P.C., 46
Scafe, Flight Lieutenant W.J., 50
Scargill, Flight Lieutenant L.H., 130
Scott, Flying Officer D.G., 69
Severn, Sergeant, 141
Shaer, Flight Sergeant J.I., 104

Shawjer, Sergeant H.K., 83
Shepherd, Flight Sergeant R.B., 77-8
Sheppard, Pilot Officer H.V.C., 142
Siegfried Line, 112
Simonson, Flying Officer E.S., 113
Sinclair, Sir Archibald, 26, *28*, 51
Sinclair, Flight Lieutenant N.D., 72,
    76
Singlehurst, Pilot Officer G.B., *73*
Skjomen Fjord, 114
Smart, Sergeant R.E., 72
Smith, Sergeant A., 63
Smith Lewis, Squadron Leader, *92*
Smylie, Group Captain G.F., 145
South Easton, 100
South Moreton, 118
South, Acting Flight Lieutenant D.,
    133
Sparkes, Flight Lieutenant J.B., 133
Spencer, Flying Officer P.J., 90
Spender, Flight Lieutenant, 10
Spezia, 14
St Dizier, 96
St Malo, 39, 41
St Nazaire, 33
St Peter, 108
St Valerie, 44
Stanlandet, 64
Stapleton, Pilot Officer H.A., 134-5
Stavanger, 68
Steele, Sergeant R., 44
Stendal, 127
Stephens, Sergeant R.A., 14
Stettin, 121, 133
Stevenson, Squadron Leader, 56
Stokenchurch, 100, 103
Stoney Cross, 102
Stopford, Flight Sergeant W.D., 118,
    120
Strain, Wing Commander, 10
Strasbourg, 45
Stratton, Wing Commander J.A.C.,
    30, 42
Streatley, 7
Suckling, Flying Officer M., *21*, 22
Sullom Voe, 143
Sutton, Pilot Officer G.N., 77
Swann, Pilot Officer J.W., 103-4
Swift, Flying Officer J.F., 29
Swinemünde, 110, 133, 134
Symes, Pilot Officer A.J.F., 143

Taffs, Flying Officer J.C., 64
Talisker, 142
Tangmere, 127

Index

Taylor, AC, 50
Taylor, Squadron Leader Alistair L., *31*, 33
Taylor, Sergeant J.H., 131
Thomas, Flying Officer, *92*
Thomas, Sergeant P.D., 83
Thompson, ASO, *117*
Thompson, Flight Sergeant H., 133
Thornaby, 143
Thorney Island, 88
Thornton, Sergeant G.T., 46
Thurso, 141
Tirpitz, 113-14, 131, *132*
Tomlinson, Flight Lieutenant P., 26
Tomlinson, Flight Sergeant R.D.C., 38
Tønder, 134
Toulon, 60
Touser the dog, *92*
Towsey, Flight Lieutenant J.S., 118
Tozer, Flight Lieutenant, *92*
Trenchard, MRAF the Viscount, 7
Trier, 127
Trieste, 49
Tromsø, 131
Trondheim, 33, 37, 38, 39, 43, 48, 72, 88
Troon, 68
Tully, Flying Officer J.L., 46
Tunis, 62
Tuttle, Wing Commander G., 10, 29, 30, *31*

Upstone, Sergeant, *92*
Urquhart, Flying Officer S.C., 100
Ursell, Sergeant H., 19

Vaenga, 50, 51
Vegesack, 46, 48
Venice, 49
Verdun, 49
Vickers, Flying Officer H.R., 121
Vienna, 62, 68
Vlasto, Pilot Officer W.T., 139

Wager, Squadron Leader, 50
Waghorn, Air Commodore D.J., 133, 134
Walker, Wing Commander D.C.B., 89
Walker, Pilot Officer G.W., 50, 51
Walker, Flight Sergeant J., 88
Wall, Flight Lieutenant A.E., 115
Wallingford, 8, 123, 133
Wanek, Sergeant, 13
Warwick, Flight Lieutenant E.V., 134-5
Watchfield, 30
Watlington, 12, 13, 103, 131
Watson, Sergeant, 58
Watson, Flight Sergeant R., 86
Watton, 29
Watts, Flight Lieutenant later Squadron Leader P.H., 84, 96, *150*
Wearn, Sergeant Pilot L.A., 141
Weaver, Flight Lieutenant later Squadron Leader J., *92*, *116*
Webb, Squadron Leader, 45
Weightman, ASO, *117*
Wesendorf, 130
West Malling, 72, 90
West, Pilot Officer F.H.S., 12
Weston Zoyland, 32, 88
Whaley, Flight Lieutenant N.P., 127
Whitaker, Pilot Officer, 48
Whitaker, Pilot Officer 'Gale', *73*
Whitby, 68
White, ACW, *92*
White, Sergeant V.B., 85
Whitehead, Flight Lieutenant, *73*
Whitehead, Squadron Leader R.V., 74
Widdington Park, 134
Wilding, Flying Officer J.A., 123
Wilhelmshaven, 23, 37, 41, 48, 51, 100
Williams, Pilot Officer J.H., 87
Wilson, Flying Officer D.E., 74
Windsor Castle, 45
Wodehouse, Flight Lieutenant A.M., 140
Woods, Flying Officer H., 122
Wooll, Flight Lieutenant, 49
Wraxall, 94
Wright, Flight Sergeant, 48
Wright, Sergeant A.G., 81

Xiezopolski, Flying Officer L., 68

Yearwood, Flying Officer F.C., 89
Young, Squadron Leader M.J.B., 55
Ystad, 110